Modern Comparative Politics Series
edited by
Peter H. Merkl
University of California,
Santa Barbara

SWEDEN
The politics of
postindustrial change

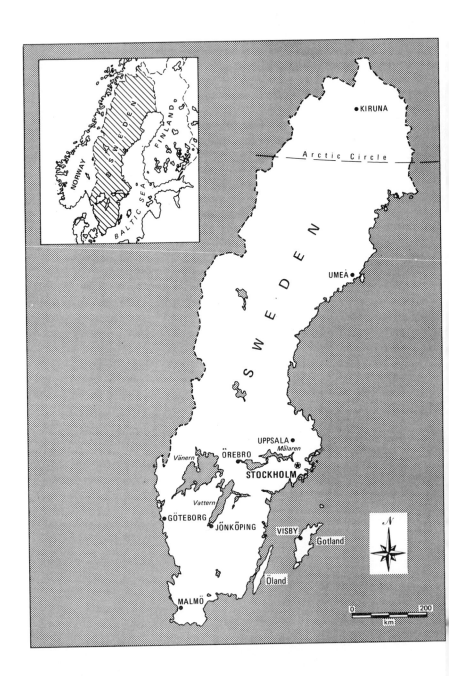

SWEDEN
The politics of
postindustrial change

M. Donald Hancock
The University of Texas

THE DRYDEN PRESS INC.
Hinsdale, Illinois

To Kay

Copyright © 1972 by The Dryden Press Inc.
Library of Congress Catalog Card Number: 75–184308
ISBN: 0–03–077770–4
Printed in the United States of America
2 3 4 5   065   9 8 7 6 5 4 3 2 1

FOREWORD TO THE SERIES

This new series in comparative politics was undertaken in response to the special needs of students, teachers, and scholars that have arisen in the last few years, needs that are no longer being satisfied by most of the materials now available. In an age when our students seem to be getting brighter and more politically aware, the teaching of comparative politics should present a greater challenge than ever before. We have seen the field come of age with numerous comparative monographs and case studies breaking new ground, and the Committee on Comparative Politics of the Social Science Research Council can look back proudly on nearly a decade of important spadework. But teaching materials have lagged behind these changing approaches to the field. Most comparative government series are either too little coordinated to make systematic use of any common methodology or too conventional in approach. Others are so restricted in scope and space as to make little more than a programmatic statement about what should be studied, thus suggesting a new scholasticism of systems theory that omits the idiosyncratic richness of the material available and tends to ignore important elements of a system for fear of being regarded too traditional in approach.

In contrast to these two extremes, the Modern Comparative Politics Series attempts to find a happy combination of rigorous, systematic methodology and the rich sources of data available to area and country specialists. The series consists of a core volume, *Modern Comparative Politics* by Peter H. Merkl, country volumes covering one or more nations, and comparative topical volumes.

Rather than narrowing the approach to only one "right" method, the core volume leaves it to the teacher to choose any of several approaches he may prefer. The authors of the country volumes are partly bound by a framework common to these volumes and the core volume, and are partly free to tailor their approaches to the idiosyncrasies of their respective countries. The emphasis in the common framework is on achieving a balance between such elements as theory and application, as well as among developmental perspectives, sociocultural aspects, the group processes, and the decision-making processes of government. It is hoped that the resulting tension between comparative approaches and politicocultural realities will enrich the teaching of comparative politics and provoke discussion at all levels from undergraduate to graduate.

The group of country volumes is supplemented by a group of analytical comparative studies. Each of these comparative volumes takes an important topic and explores it cross-nationally. Some of these topics are covered in a more limited way in the country volumes, but many find their first expanded treatment in the comparative volumes—and all can be expected to break new scholarly ground.

The ideas embodied in the series owe much to the many persons whose names are cited in the footnotes of the core volume. Although they are far too numerous to mention here, a special debt of spiritual paternity is acknowledged to Harry Eckstein, Gabriel A. Almond, Carl J. Friedrich, Sidney Verba, Lucian W. Pye, Erik H. Erikson, Eric C. Bellquist, R. Taylor Cole, Otto Kirchheimer, Seymour M. Lipset, Joseph La Palombara, Samuel P. Huntington, Cyril E. Black, and many others, most of whom are probably quite unaware of their contribution.

Santa Barbara, California   P. H. M.

PREFACE

Two perspectives on modern Swedish society permeate this book. One emphasizes the consensual norms of moderation and compromise that have distinguished the Swedish experience in the past and continue to characterize social and political relations among most of the population. The second stresses the emergence of a new critical consciousness, especially among the nation's youth and intellectuals, which has accompanied the New Left-radical liberal debate in the 1960s. Since these dual perspectives correspond to the realities of contemporary Sweden, neither can be safely ignored nor depreciated. A systematic analysis of Swedish politics thus requires their simultaneous assessment.

Tension between norms supporting the established pluralist system and critical consciousness among a vocal minority distinguishes not only Sweden's transition to postindustrial society but sociopolitical change in other advanced states as well. Contradictions between the performance of industrial-welfare systems and their unfulfilled potentials have helped generate resurgent ideological controversy on a global scale. In the particular case of Sweden the new radicalism has served as the cutting edge of reform, while diffused tenets of restraint and compromise on the part of national leaders will conceivably—though not inevitably—help channel aspirations for change into constructive patterns of future transformation. Transcending the conflict between opposing forces of stability and change are peculiar structural features of the Swedish system such as the office of the ombudsmen that seek, through continuous adjustments, to reconcile them.

I do not mean to imply that Sweden will, with certainty, resolve the tensions of the postindustrial era. The historical record provides a promising precedent of radical reform, but it does not justify future complacency. In the present age of discontinuity and uncertainty, the past provides no certain guidelines for tomorrow.

For these reflections and my interpretation of modern Swedish politics I assume personal responsibility. To those who have provided intellectual stimulation and essential research support in the evolution of this volume, however, I wish to express my gratitude. Among them are Professors Dankwart A. Rustow, Gideon Sjoberg, Olof Ruin, Nils Andrén, and the late Otto Kirchheimer; Bengt Rösiö, former Swedish Consul-General in Houston, and numerous officials in the Foreign Ministry in Stockholm; and colleagues in my department at the University of Texas. A special note of appreciation is due Peter Merkl, whose helpful comments on an earlier draft helped clarify many of my thoughts. I acknowledge gratefully the Social Science Foundation and Department of International Relations in Denver, Colorado, for their permission to incorporate in this volume sections of a previous study of mine on Swedish politics (*Sweden: A Multiparty System in Transition?* Denver: Monograph Series in World Affairs, 1968). May my wife, Kay, and my son, Erik, know that I have labored ultimately for them.

Austin, Texas   M.D.H.
January 1972

CONTENTS

TABLES AND FIGURES

SWEDEN
The politics of
postindustrial change

INTRODUCTION
MODERNITY AND
POLITICAL CHANGE

In an era of revolutionary upheaval, Sweden stands as an exemplary model of progressive sociopolitical transformation. Since the beginning of the century Sweden has succeeded in combining rapid industrialization with the attainment of an effective pluralist democracy. Equally significant, Sweden is today one of a handful of nations undergoing the transition to postindustrial society.

A primary purpose of this volume is to explore the historical, socioeconomic, and political factors that distinguish the Swedish experience. My underlying objective, however, is theoretical. Viewed in comparison with the Nordic states and other advanced industrial-welfare societies, Sweden assumes significance beyond the interest of a configurative study. One of the world's most advanced and stable nations, Sweden illustrates important common features of modernity.

Accordingly, I shall seek to appraise the Swedish political system within a theoretical context that is applicable to all industrialized states. The basis for my analytical framework is provided by the modernization concept. Among the nations of Western Europe and North America, modernization encompasses continuing processes of economic, social, and political change. The effect of such changes may have major consequences for the future of politics in what colleagues and I have described elsewhere as the postwelfare state.[1]

---

[1] M. Donald Hancock and Gideon Sjoberg (eds.), *Politics in the Post-Welfare State: Responses to the New Individualism* (New York: Columbia University Press, 1972).

1

MODERNIZATION IN COMPARATIVE ANALYSIS

The proliferation of political modernization and development studies in recent decades reflects the fundamental transformation of the international political system since the end of World War II. Such studies constitute a response to the intellectual as well as policy-oriented needs to fashion new analytical approaches to appraise problems of industrialization and nation-building in former colonial territories and older nations such as those in Latin America. The cumulative effect of postwar attempts to expand the horizon of political inquiry has been to emphasize universal reference points in political behavior. To the extent that modernization is both an historical experience shared by many nations and the goal of most leaders in the new nations, modernization is a global phenomenon. The modernization-development concept therefore provides—in contrast to the static-descriptive orientation of earlier traditions of comparative scholarship—a common analytical framework that facilitates systematic cross-national generalizations.

Admittedly little consensus exists on precise definitions of modernization and development. Some scholars use the terms interchangeably, while others view development as a specialized aspect of the broader modernization phenomenon. For present purposes I shall refrain from any such dichotomy in favor of a single inclusive definition of modernization. By modernization I mean processes of economic, social, and political change by which man acquires enhanced control over his physical, social, and individual environments.[2] Empirical indexes of modernization in a given political system include the nation's level of industrialization, national and per capita wealth, the application of advanced technological and scientific knowledge, the scope of social mobilization and political participation, the capacity of political authorities to make and execute collective policy decisions, and individual freedom from physical and economic insecurity.[3] These are meant to

[2] This definition of modernization is derived from Dankwart A. Rustow, *A World of Nations* (Washington, D.C.: Brookings Institution, 1967), pp. 3–5, and C. E. Black, *The Dynamics of Modernization* (New York: Harper and Row, 1966), p. 7.

[3] Any set of indexes, including this one, is inevitably somewhat arbitrary. I have, for example, omitted cultural attributes of modernity on the grounds that they are least subject to a common operational definition. Moreover, ostensibly objective criteria such as the scope of social mobilization and political participation are subject to differing evaluations—especially in light of conflicting ideological perspectives. Thus many Western observers would deny that elections in the Soviet Union are meaningful manifestations of mass participation in politics

be strictly quantitative measures of modernization; I shall consider some qualitative implications below.

The scope of the existing literature on modernization ranges from the configurative analysis of sociopolitical change in specific countries to broadly comparative assessments of modernization as a universal aspiration.[4] Despite widely divergent approaches to the analysis of the modernization process, inherent in the very concept is a distinction between stages or levels of modernization. "Premodern" societies share characteristics such as predominantly agrarian economies, ascriptive value systems, "fused" decision-making structures, and forms of political authority that are sanctioned by time and tradition. "Transitional" or modernizing nations, in contrast, are those that are undergoing processes of industrialization, bureaucratization, secularization, social integration, and social mobilization. In such societies achievement displaces ascription as the primary criterion of recruitment and status, and political authority becames institutionalized in structurally differentiated offices and groups (such as the military). "Modern" systems, meanwhile, include the affluent, industrialized, and highly structured nations of North America, Europe, and parts of the British Commonwealth. Modernity embraces, therefore, the highest stage of man's control over his collective and individual environments.

Such distinctions between premodern, transitional, and modern nations do not imply an inevitable chain of sociopolitical evo-

---

on the grounds that they deny the voter an effective choice among alternative candidates or political programs. Conversely, orthodox Marxist-Leninists would argue that elections in the West merely mask class rule by the bourgeoisie. In utilizing indexes of modernity, therefore, it is imperative that the social scientist explicitly state his underlying value premises. My own view is that the crucial variable in determining effective participation is the working relation between the claims of the collectivity for conformity and the capacity of the individual to make meaningful choices in politics as in career opportunities and consumption. Depending on the degree of collective control over individual behavior in a given society, one can thus distinguish between authoritarian and libertarian variants of modernity.

[4] Country monographs include Lucian W. Pye, *Politics, Personality and Nation-Building: Burma's Search for Identity* (New Haven, Conn.: Yale University Press, 1962), Myron Weiner, *Party Politics in India* (Princeton, N.J.: Princeton University Press, 1957), and the individual chapters in Gabriel Almond and James Coleman (eds.), *The Politics of the Developing Areas* (Princeton, N.J.: Princeton University Press, 1960). Among those who have approached modernization from a global perspective are Rustow, Black, Samuel Huntington, *Political Order in Changing Societies* (New Haven, Conn.: Yale University Press, 1968), David E. Apter, *The Politics of Modernization* (Chicago: The University of Chicago Press, 1965), and Karl Deutsch, "Social Mobilization and Political Development," *American Political Science Review*, 55 (1961), 493–514.

lution. Few social scientists would maintain, for instance, that the modernizing nations of Africa, the Middle East, Asia, and Latin America will inevitably become close replicas of today's modern systems. Moreover, as Samuel Huntington has cogently argued, modernization is not a unilineal process; nations may decay as well as attain new levels of modernizing change.[5]

Nevertheless, the already modern industrial nations are commonly posited as empirical models against which the achievements (or lack of them) of premodern or transitional societies are measured. In their comparative assessment of political culture in five countries, for example, Gabriel Almond and Sidney Verba view the "civic culture" of the United States and Great Britain as the most advanced synthesis of political attitudes, beliefs, and values extant in the contemporary world.[6] In comparison with this ideal type, the political cultures of the three other countries included in their study—Germany, Italy, and Mexico—are characterized as deficient in important civic attributes. Implied in such a conceptualization is that modern nations—in this case, the United States and Britain—have attained a pinnacle of modernity beyond which no significant change is envisioned.

THE RELATIVITY OF MODERNITY

Supporting this preception of politics in modern nations is the "end-of-ideology" thesis advanced by such social scientists as S. M. Lipset, Daniel Bell, Herbert Tingsten, and Manfred Friedrich.[7] Emphasizing the decline of traditional forms of ideological conflict in advanced societies—such as earlier political debates on government intervention in the economy or the need for welfare services—they concluded that American and Western European societies had entered an era of elite-mass consensus on public policy. Henceforth conflict would be restricted to largely peripheral issues of leadership style, policy priorities, and emphasis.

Events in recent years have revealed the fallacy of this prediction. Premature at best, the end-of-ideology argument has been

[5] Huntington, *Political Order in Changing Societies.*
[6] Gabriel Almond and Sidney Verba, *The Civic Culture* (Boston: Little Brown and Company, 1965).
[7] S. M. Lipset, *Political Man* (New York: Anchor Books, 1963), chap. 13; Daniel Bell, *The End of Ideology* (rev. ed.), (New York: Collier Books, 1961), especially pp. 393–402; Herbert Tingsten, *Från idéer till idyll* (Stockholm: P. A. Norstedt & Söners Förlag, 1966); and Manfred Friedrich, *Opposition ohne Alternative?* (Cologne: Verlag Wissenschaft und Politik, 1963).

patently challenged by the emergence of new forms of ideological controversy. From Berkeley to Paris, Berlin, and Stockholm, dissident students, workers, minority groups, and intellectuals have emerged as outspoken critics of the existing sociopolitical order. Through confrontations with public authorities, street demonstrations, general strikes, and renewed stress on ideological agitation in electoral campaigns, radicals on both extremes of the political spectrum have expressed their growing dissatisfaction with basis aspects of contemporary industrial-pluralist society. The result is a marked politicization—and even polarization—of major groups in society.

The resurgence of ideological conflict is but the most dramatic evidence of continuing change in the ostensibly modernized systems. Beneath the surface of overt controversy, forces of fundamental social transformation have gained increased momentum. Technological innovation and new scientific discoveries, combined with the emergence of problems of urban decay and pollution, point to a future that is simultaneously promising and foreboding.

The implications of these many facets of change in advanced industrial-political systems are clear. Modernity is a relative concept, with present economic, social, and political patterns in the advanced nations representing no finite end of the modernization process. Like transitional societies in the third world, modern systems confront continuing demands of modernization—albeit on a significantly different level. In both cases the future course of modernization is by no means determinate. Political decay in transitional societies may well find its parallel in the incapacity of advanced nations to adjust to ongoing domestic and international change—triggering instances of violent upheaval such as the abortive 1968 revolution in France and ghetto riots in the United States.

POSTINDUSTRIAL MODERNIZATION

Given the relativity of modernity, contemporary manifestations of change in the advanced nations pose a major challenge to political analysis. To comprehend the possible consequences of such change, it is imperative to speculate intelligently about the possible future of modern industrial society. If it is true that what man thinks about the future will to a certain extent determine that future, greater awareness of the range of options open to modern man for structuring his environment can facilitate a rational choice among those options.[8]

In recent years a new genre of "futurology" literature has emerged, which testifies to the growing interest among scholars in assessing the effects of current trends—primarily technological—on future socioeconomic relations. Examples include Herman Kahn's *Toward the Year 2000* and Zbigniew Brzezinski's *Between Two Ages*.[9] As we argue in our own treatment of the postwelfare state, however, additional perspectives are necessary. Insufficient emphasis has been given to the political dimensions of contemporary processes of change, particularly in a cross-cultural context, and too many social scientists have tended to restrict their predictions to projections from the present into the future. What is required for more comprehensive analysis of the future of politics, therefore, is a broader comparative perspective that emphasizes the potential for discontinuity as well as continuity in modern industrial society.[10]

The modernization concept provides a basis for such a cross-national analytical framework. In that the modernization approach explicitly builds on a dynamic view of politics—that is, the cumulative acquisition of greater control by man over his physical, social, and individual environments—it serves as a useful point of departure in constructing alternative images of future sociopolitical relations.

Embracing multiple dimensions of environmental control, the modernization process contains an obvious contradiction. Collective demands for control—for example, demands for political obedience and conformity in social behavior—can conflict (and often have conflicted) with simultaneous demands by individuals to determine their own destinies. Throughout the preindustrial and industrial phases of modernization, this tension has usually been resolved in favor of dominance by the collectivity (that is, by the national political community or subsystems thereof). Regardless of whether the modernization process has led to a violent or a peaceful transition from one socioeconomic and political system

---

[8] Gideon Sjoberg, M. Donald Hancock, and Orion White, Jr., *Politics in the Post-Welfare State: A Comparison of the United States and Sweden* (Bloomington, Ind.: Carnegie Seminar on Political and Administrative Development, 1967), pp. 2–4. This theme is expanded in Hancock and Sjoberg, "Epilogue," *Politics in the Post-Welfare State: Responses to the New Individualism.*

[9] Herman Kahn, *Toward the Year 2000* (New York: Macmillan, 1967) and Zbigniew Brzezinski, *Between Two Ages: America's Role in the Technetronic Era* (New York: The Viking Press, 1970).

[10] Hancock and Sjoberg, *Politics in the Post-Welfare State: Responses to the New Individualism.*

to another, successive generations of leaders in today's advanced nations have utilized the enhanced capabilities of modernizing change to extend collective control over nature and the domestic system itself.

As a major consequence of modernization, individual citizens have undeniably acquired major advantages. Through mass literacy, the diffusion of national wealth, and the extended scope of political participation in the advanced nations, a majority of citizens enjoy greater individual security and freedom than their forebears in preindustrial society. Yet even in the pluralist democracies of Western Europe and North America, such freedom has remained relative. Individuals have controlled their choice of occupation, style of life, and political preferences only within the limits imposed by general conformity with collective norms. Formal as well as informal sanctions—ranging from the threat of imprisonment to the internalization of the prevailing value system through processes of socialization—have functioned as effective restraints on excessive individual deviance from accepted behavior patterns.

As modern industrial systems continue to sustain economic growth and achieve mass affluence, postindustrial modernization becomes an historic possibility. Used by numerous social scientists to describe the emerging era of economic and social relations in the United States and much of Western Europe, a postindustrial society can be defined as one in which the primacy of capital accumulation and industrial production yields to the potential primacy of redistribution—of wealth, material goods, political influence, and social status. As an important corollary of postindustrial modernization, the inherent contradiction between collective and individual claims for control has accordingly assumed new dimensions.

Modernity has generated unprecedented problems—such as ecological decay, high population densities, and the need for new systems of mass transportation—that require even more comprehensive collective action than in the past. Yet mass affluence simultaneously makes possible greater individual autonomy from the larger group. In place of the earlier functional requirement that individuals be socialized or forced to accept collective priorities on behalf of modernizing goals, the individual is increasingly free to disregard such pressures for conformity. Hippie subcultures in the United States and elsewhere are but one manifestation of the new option that individuals can now exercise to "drop out" of the established socioeconomic system. At the same time other groups—such as ethnic minorities, lower paid industrial workers, and women—have become more conscious of their relative lack of economic security and social status vis-à-vis more privileged groups in society. Hence they have raised demands for a proportionate share of material advantages or social opportunities that modernity has already provided other strata.

These coterminous facets of postindustrial modernization can lead to a theoretical range of alternative futures. Given the tension between opposing claims for more extensive environmental control by the collectivity, the assertion of new forms of individualism, and demands by minority groups for a more equitable distribution of economic advantages and political influence, the future course of change is unlikely to involve a simple continuation of contemporary political processes and structures. If leaders in modern industrial societies are unable or unwilling to respond to contemporary forces of postindustrial modernization, the result could be violent confrontation that can threaten the viability of the political system itself. Conversely, conscious efforts to channel postindustrial modernization can facilitate a positive synthesis between enhanced capabilities for environmental control on both the collective and individual levels.

The potential course of postindustrial modernization can be conceptualized along the following continuum:

Regressive Change	System Maintaining Change	System Transforming Change

Regressive change would involve the breakdown of existing political structures or the inability of the political system to satisfy the new policy demands generated by postindustrial modernization (such as that for ecological control). Transforming change, in contrast, would encompass sustained policy and structural adaptation to accommodate such requirements. Between these extremes lies system maintaining change, which can be conceived of as either *ad hoc*, fragmentary measures or a coherent program of sociopolitical conservatism to shore up the existing political system.[11]

[11] My definition of regressive and transforming change corresponds approximately to Manfred Halpern's distinction between incoherent and coherent change. "Incoherent transformation," he writes, "turns encounters into chaos, renders dialogue impossible, and obscures, thus deepening injustices." In contrast coherent change consists of four components—"new forms of consciousness, creativity, institutionalized power and justice . . ."—that "together constitute an enduring capacity to generate and absorb persistent transformation." Halpern, "A Redefinition of the Revolutionary Situation," *Journal of International Affairs*, 23 (1969), 55–58.

Each of these variants of postindustrial change provides a different image of the future. None of the variants is predetermined, nor can one assume that any is irreversible. Transforming change can yield to maintaining change once given or projected levels of modernization are attained. Similarly, the threat of political disintegration wrought by regressive change may provide the impetus for transformation. Whether a particular nation will exemplify regressive, maintaining, or transforming change will depend on a variety of policy variables. The most important of these would seem to include a nation's socioeconomic capabilities, the scope of elite-mass consensus on fundamental sociopolitical values, and the attitudes of the politically influential toward system change.[12] International factors will also determine in part the prospects of postindustrial modernization. A nation that has extensive foreign military commitments, for example, might confront greater obstacles to achieving transforming change than one that has few or none.

IMPLICATIONS FOR ANALYSIS

As an analytical framework, the concept of postindustrial modernization raises important methodological and normative considerations. First, the fact that it emphasizes the ubiquity of political *change* underscores the necessity for process analysis. As postindustrial modernization may assume a variety of forms, the student of politics must be attuned to the possibility of sharp break between the present and the future. The fact that much of the resurgence of ideological controversy in contemporary advanced nations has arisen from contradictions between proclaimed sociopolitical values and actual system performance suggests the methodological utility of a dialectical approach to the study of postindustrial modernization. Thus speculation about the future of modern society must rely not only on empirical knowledge of *established* political patterns but also on emerging forces of opposition—such as militant minority and student movements—that seek to transform existing systems. By analyzing the source and nature of tensions between "establishment" and "antisystem" groups, the political scientist can more readily appraise prospects

---

[12] Weighing these factors depends more on careful judgment than precise measures. I shall expand on these variables and their relations in Chapter Eleven below.

of change than if he restricts his inquiry to forces of stability and system maintenance.[13]

Second, from a normative perspective, the indeterminate course of postindustrial modernization requires a reassessment of the role of social scientists. As an empirical definition the concept of modernization is ethically neutral. The possible effects of postindustrial modernization, on the other hand, involve qualitative evaluation. If transforming change by the collectivity is accompanied by enhanced coercive capability to enforce uniformity of political attitudes among the general populace, liberterian values will suffer. Through the use of sophisticated surveillance and control techniques, already made possible by modern technology, a postindustrial society could institutionalize a more extensive degree of totalitarianism than even the National Socialist and Stalinist precedents. At the opposite extreme, efforts to attain transformation wholly on behalf of atomistic individualism could initiate regressive change with respect to the national political community as a whole. In both cases a majority of citizens would suffer a diminution of individual security that modernity presently provides or promises.

To help avoid such desultory consequences of postindustrial change, the social scientist bears a joint responsibility with political and other leaders in society. While he should continually strive for more precise, systematic knowledge of accordance with the basic principles of scientific inquiry, the social scientist cannot remain impassive in his awareness of the sociopolitical implications of his findings. Instead, he will conceivably have to assume more of a participant role in the continuing process of modernization—whether as social critic, policy adviser, or political activitist.

THE CASE OF SWEDEN

Postindustrial modernization provides the analytical framework and central theme for this study. Until the advent of industrialization in the latter part of the nineteenth century, Sweden was a relatively poor, socially immobile, and oligarchical political system. Since then Sweden has undergone simultaneous processes of

---

[13] For a detailed explanation of countersystem analysis, see Gideon Sjoberg and Leonard D. Cain, "Negative Values, Countersystem Models, and the Analysis of Social Systems," in Herman Turk and Richard Simpson (eds.), *The Sociologies of Talcott Parsons and George C. Homans* (Indianapolis, Ind.: Bobbs-Merrill, 1971).

economic, social, and political modernization. Today Sweden is a highly industrialized, affluent, welfare state. In light of the domestic cultural-political debate and recent policy initiatives, Sweden appears to have entered the postindustrial era as a leading empirical example of system transforming change.

Although it is impossible to generalize about the future of postindustrial society from the experience of a single nation, Sweden nevertheless serves as a useful mirror with which to compare change in other advanced systems. To facilitate such comparisons I have incorporated data from other modern states, particularly Scandinavia and the United States, throughout the study. In my concluding chapter, I shall return to a broader cross-cultural perspective.

ONE
SWEDEN IN PERSPECTIVE
Political, economic, and social modernization

Sweden, Lars Gustafsson has observed, is a singular country.[1] Without domestic revolution or foreign invasion Sweden evolved in the brief span of half a century from a country with a predominantly agrarian economy and oligarchial system of government to an industrialized pluralist democracy. Political stability has become a national characteristic, epitomized by such concepts as the "politics of compromise" and a "working multiparty system."[2] In foreign affairs Sweden has remained at peace as a neutral nation since 1814.

As a case study of postindustrial modernization Sweden provides a mosaic of apparent contradictions. A constitutional monarch reigns over a parliamentary system of government. Despite political fragmentation among five established parties—ranging from the Left Party-Communists through the Social Democrats, the Center (Agrarians), and the Liberals to the Moderate Unity (Conservative) party—the Swedish Social Democrats have maintained one-party dominance of the national cabinet for nearly

[1] Lars Gustafsson, *The Public Dialogue in Sweden* (Stockholm: P. A. Norstedt & Söners Förlag, 1964), p. 8.
[2] Dankwart A. Rustow, *The Politics of Compromise* (Princeton, N.J.: Princeton University Press, 1955) and Rustow, "Scandinavia: Working Multiparty Systems," in Sigmund Neumann (ed.), *Modern Political Parties* (Chicago: University of Chicago Press, 1956).

13

four decades. Elaborate welfare services are sustained by an economic system that remains 90 percent in private hands.

Sweden's success in synthesizing diverse historical traditions, political structures, and socioeconomic forces is a product of domestic as well as international factors. Prominent among these are geography, population characteristics, and economic resources.

GEOGRAPHY, POPULATION, AND RESOURCES

Encompassing the heart of the Scandinavian peninsula, Sweden is bordered on the west by Norway and is separated only by the narrow Öresund strait from Denmark to the southwest. In the tundra regions of the far northwest Sweden shares 586 kilometers (365 miles) of sparsely settled frontier above the Arctic circle with Finland. These four nations—along with more remote Iceland and the Danish possession of Greenland—comprise the Scandinavian regional subsystem.

All of the Nordic states manifest broadly similar sociopolitical, economic, and legal systems. Overwhelmingly Protestant, the Scandinavian nations are at the same time characterized by secularized political and social culture. Language barriers within Scandinavia are minimal, with Swedish, Norwegian, and Danish embodying a basic linguistic affinity that facilitates communication. Among the Scandinavians only the Finns speak a distinct language—which is related etymologically to such Finno-Ugric languages as Estonian and Hungarian—but most Finns learn Swedish, as it is Finland's second official language.[3]

Located on the same latitude as Alaska and Siberia, the four principal Scandinavian countries are geographically removed from direct proximity to major world trade routes and contemporary centers of conflict. Through elaborate economic, transportation, and political links, however, they are highly integrated in the international community. Their aggregate trade—including high-grade iron ore, fish, timber products, quality furniture, and automobiles—comprises 5.2 percent of the world's total.[4] Sweden,

[3] The persistence of Swedish linguistic and cultural influence in Finland is a product of the historical union of the countries that lasted until 1809. Today approximately 8 percent of the Finnish population speaks Swedish as its native language.

[4] Nordic Council, *Yearbook of Nordic Statistics* (Stockholm: Nordic Council, 1969), p. 17.

Norway, Denmark, and Iceland are full members of the European Free Trade Association, while Finland is an associate member. Connected by air service to virtually all countries, Scandinavia boasts a major airline system of its own (SAS), which is jointly owned by the three central Scandinavian states. Three of the Nordic nations—Denmark, Norway, and Iceland—belong to the North Atlantic Treaty Organization. A Norwegian (Trygvie Lie) and a Swede (Dag Hammarskjöld) served as the first two Secretaries-General of the United Nations. Two eminent Swedish civil servants have represented the United Nations in international mediation efforts in the Middle East: Count Folke Bernadotte, who was assassinated in Palestine in 1948, and Gunnar Jarring, who was appointed in 1970 to help ameliorate the Arab-Israeli conflict. All of the Scandinavian countries have been actively involved in United Nations peacekeeping operations along the Suez and in Africa.

Among the Nordic nations Sweden is the largest and most populated. With an area of nearly 450,000 square kilometers (173,423 square miles) Sweden is approximately the size of California. Finland is second with an area of 337,000 square kilometers (117,970 square miles) followed by Norway with 324,000 square kilometers (119,240 square miles) and Denmark with 43,000 square kilometers (16,576 square miles). Sweden's population of 7,918,000 is nearly double that of Denmark (4,870,000) and Finland (4,446,000). Norway is the least populated of the four nations with 3,819,000. Denmark's population density of 111 inhabitants per square kilometer, however, is significantly higher than Sweden's 19, Finland's 14, and Norway's 12.

Over 50 percent of Sweden's population is concentrated in Götaland in the southern third of the country. Warmed by the Gulf stream and more accessible than the rest of the country to international markets and sources of raw materials, Götaland is the center of Sweden's industrial and agricultural production. Here, too, are located the nation's three largest cities. Founded in the thirteenth century as a fortress town to guard the inland lakes against enemy encroachments from the Baltic, Stockholm—Sweden's capital—has a population of 1,275,000. Second in size is Göteborg on the west coast, which is Sweden's principal port city, with a population of 637,000. Malmö, situated across the Öresund sound from the Danish capital of Copenhagen, has 421,070 inhabitants.

Like her Scandinavian neighbors Sweden displays a high degree of social homogeneity. Except for nearly 10,000 Lapps in the

Arctic region, many of whom migrate annually across northern Scandinavia, Sweden has no marked ethnic minorities. Approximately 30,000 Finnish-speaking Swedes live in Norrland, but they are fully integrated into the national cultural and political system. Virtually all Swedes speak a common language, albeit with sometimes pronounced regional differences. Moreover, most are at least nominal members of the state Lutheran church. Less than 5 percent of the population are Catholics or members of dissenting Protestant sects.

The Swedes inhabit a land of scenic contrasts and abundant natural resources. From the gently rolling, fertile plains of the agricultural provinces of Skåne and Bohus in the south to the mountainous timber and mining districts in the north and northwest, Sweden presents a variegated landscape of compelling beauty. Over 8 percent of Sweden's area consists of lakes and waterways. The largest, Lake Vännern in the center of Götaland, is 5585 square kilometers (2156 square miles) in size. Off the southeastern coast in the Baltic are located Sweden's two principal islands, Gotland and Öland. Pine forests, lining many of the country's lakes and rivers and shrouding more than 93,000 kilometers (57,800 miles) of winding roadways, cover over half of the country.

Natural attributes of forests and water constitute in turn important resources for Sweden's contemporary economy. Pulp and timber production totaled nearly 54 million cubic meters in 1967, while coastal and deep-sea fishing yielded 514,554 tons (1966). Along with agriculture, the nation's timber and fishing industries contribute approximately 6 percent of Sweden's gross domestic product. Over a thousand power stations convert the energy of rivers and artificial lakes into nearly 10,000 kilowatts of electrical power annually.

Augmenting these resources are rich deposits of iron ore and other minerals. Deposits estimated at over two billion tons of the highest grade iron ore available in Europe are mined in Norrbotten province at a rate of 28 million tons a year. (Deficient in domestic supplies of coal, Sweden must export much of the ore for processing in Germany and France.) In addition, Sweden claims significant veins of ferro alloys, pyrites, fire clay, zinc, silver, and lead.

In combination these factors—geographic insularity, social homogeneity, and abundant natural resources—help explain Sweden's past and present course of modernization. Buffered from direct involvement in continental warfare since the Napoleonic wars, Sweden has pursued an uninterrupted course of domestic change for the past 160 years. Unencumbered by ethnic, linguistic, or religious cleavages that have disrupted development in many other areas of the world, the Swedish system has achieved a largely harmonious transition to modernity.

POLITICAL MODERNIZATION

Enhanced sociopolitical control over executive decision processes —a basic tenet of political modernization—was institutionalized in Sweden through the gradual transformation from the mid-nineteenth century onward of a traditional monarchy into a parliamentary democracy. In more or less parallel steps throughout Scandinavia this process was marked by the emergence of multiparty systems, the extension of suffrage rights, and the introduction of ministerial responsibility.

While Sweden has been receptive to the influence of major political and philosophical currents from abroad, particularly the importation of liberal and socialist thought, the nation's relative geographic isolation has conditioned the evolution of a "system of government [that is] basically the result of indigenous developments and experience."[5] The culmination, however, closely resembles modern parliamentary patterns elsewhere. Similar to the British and Benelux models of parliamentary government, the Swedish monarch performs largely symbolic functions as formal head of state. Effective executive authority, meanwhile, rests with the prime minister and members of the national cabinet who are responsible for their tenure in office to a majority in the Riksdag (parliament). The same pattern prevails throughout the rest of Scandinavia except that a popularly elected president serves as head of state in Finland and Iceland.

Modernization occurred in Sweden within the boundaries of a nation-state that dates from the sixteenth century. Until then Swedish history was virtually indistinguishable from that of Scandinavia as a whole. During the Viking era (700–1000 A.D.)—when Scandinavian merchant-warriors settled Iceland and Greenland and pillaged much of England, Normandy, and the Baltic coast—incipient monarchical kingdoms gradually displaced earlier regional tribal communities. Primarily as a result of Christianiza-

[5] Nils Andrén, *Svensk statskunskap* (Stockholm: Bokförlaget Liber, 1963), p. 11. Unless otherwise noted, all translations from the Swedish are my own.

tion, which began in the tenth century in Denmark and spread by the end of the twelfth to the remainder of Scandinavia, the Nordic kingdoms were simultaneously incorporated into the Western cultural community. Sweden (together with its eastern province of Finland), Norway, and Denmark were then united in 1397 under Danish domination in a common monarchy known as the Kalmar Union. Swedish hostility to Danish rule broke out in a peasant uprising in 1434, which was joined by the nobility and led to the convocation of the first Riksdag in 1435, and intermittent dynastical wars from the 1490s onward. Under the leadership of Gustaf Eriksson Vasa, a nobleman who allied himself with the Hanseatic League against Denmark, the Swedes succeeded in 1521–1523 in asserting their independence. Elected king by the Riksdag in 1523, Gustaf Vasa (who was crowned as Gustaf I) proclaimed the Reformation in Sweden in 1527 and proceeded to establish the legal-political basis for a unified nation-state.[6]

Through increased military strength and territorial aggrandizement Sweden emerged during the next two centuries as a major European power. Successive wars with Russia resulted in Swedish annexation of Estonia in 1595, the southeastern coast of the Gulf of Finland in 1617, and Livonia in 1621. In 1630 King Gustaf II Adolf (Gustavus Adolphus) led Sweden into the Thirty Years War on the continent. Although Gustaf II Adolf was killed in combat, the war led to a further extension of the Swedish empire with the acquisition of various north German territories under terms of the Treaty of Westphalia (1648). As a consequence of war with Denmark in 1657, Sweden extended its immediate southern boundary to include the provinces of Skåne, Blekinge, Halland, and Bohus.

As Russia and the north German states gained in strength, Sweden's Baltic hegemony began to disintegrate. The north German territories were ceded to Hannover and Prussia by 1720. The Great Northern War of 1709–1721, in which the armies of King Karl XII were decisively defeated in Russia, ended with Russian absorption of the Baltic countries and portions of southeastern Finland. Russia gained additional Finnish territory in 1741 and, following the Treaty of Tilsit with Napoleonic France in 1807, annexed Finland altogether in a war with Sweden in 1808–1809.

In compensation for Sweden's loss of Finland, the victorious anti-French coalition sanctioned the transfer of Norway from Denmark to Sweden in the Treaty of Kiel in 1815. Sweden conceded Norwegian demands for a separate constitution and an au-

---

[6] On the role of law as a unifying force in Sweden, see Chapter Nine below.

tonomous legislative-administrative system, but controlled executive and foreign policy in the new Swedish-Norwegian Union by virtue of the monarch's authority to designate the Norwegian viceroy (who was equivalent to prime minister). In 1884 the Swedish king recognized the principle of parliamentary government in Norway when he agreed to appoint the viceroy in accordance with majority preference in the Norwegian national assembly (the *Storting*). Continued Norwegian resentment of Swedish dominance finally led to the peaceful dissolution of the Union in 1905 when Norway declared its independence and established its own monarchy. With this step Sweden was reduced to its contemporary national boundaries.

Domestically Sweden experienced five major constitutional settlements—representing recurring cycles of monarchical absolutism and parliamentary supremacy—following its own assertion of independence in the sixteenth century.[7] Limited monarchical rule prevailed until 1682 when King Karl XI joined with the clergy, peasants, and the incipient burgher class against the nobility to establish a system of royal absolutism. In 1719, following the death of Karl XII, the Swedish parliament adopted a new constitution that considerably weakened executive prerogatives and introduced the so-called Era of Liberty. During the ensuing five decades of parliamentary predominance, Sweden's first political parties—known as the "Caps" and the "Hats"—emerged in the Riksdag. Lacking a coherent organization and political program, neither faction was a party in the modern sense. Instead each was distinguished by conflicting views on foreign policy: the Hats sought to oppose Russia and recapture the lost Baltic territories, while the Caps favored conciliation with the Russian empire.

The Age of Liberty came to an end in 1772 when King Gustaf III staged a peaceful *coup d'état* that restored the monarch's right to veto parliamentary legislation. A second coup in 1789, which abolished the king's traditional advisory council, further centralized monarchical rule. Royal absolutism persisted even after Gustaf III's assassination in 1792 under his successor, King Gustaf IV Adolf.

In reaction to Sweden's loss of Finland to Russia in 1808–1809, an alliance of nobles and military officers deposed Gustaf IV Adolf in a bloodless palace coup in 1809. To restrict the autocratic power of the monarchy the Riksdag promulgated a new

---

[7] The standard reference for the study of Swedish constitutional history is Nils Herlitz, *Grunddragen av det svenska statskickets historia*, 5th ed. (Stockholm: Norstedts, 1959).

constitution and elected Jean-Baptiste Bernadotte, a French marshall, regent in 1810. He subsequently ruled as King Karl XIV Johan from 1818 to 1844. The adoption of the constitution of 1809, the second oldest written constitution in the world, initiated the evolution of Sweden's modern political system.

According to the original constitutional documents, political authority was divided between the monarchy and a four estate parliament comprising the nobility, the clergy, the burghers, and the peasantry. But opposition to the dominance of the nobility coupled with the first stirrings of industrialization, and the gradual diffusion of liberal doctrines from the continent and America prompted the reorganization of the Riksdag in 1865–1866 into a bicameral legislature. The result of this reform was the emergence of sharp political differences between the two houses. The upper house or first chamber—to some extent a prolongation of the former Estate of the Nobility—was dominated by the wealthier strata of Sweden's population, while preponderant power in the lower house (second chamber) lay in the hands of the farmers.[8] The king retained for the time being most of his executive and legislative prerogatives, with parliament then posing no direct challenge to his authority. Douglas Verney offers as a probable explanation of this phenomenon the "harmony of interests of the *herrar* [nobility] and the King in opposition to the farmers.[9]

Antagonism between the two houses during the latter part of the nineteenth century was heightened by a persistent suffrage controversy. Proposals calling for a revision of property qualifications that circumscribed the then extremely limited right of suffrage had been voiced as early as the 1860s. Agitation for electoral reform became a critical issue in the 1890s, coinciding with Sweden's industrialization and the rise of embryonic political parties within the Riksdag and among disenfranchised elements of the working class and the rural population.

Demands to extend the basis of parliamentary representation, advocated by both the newly founded Liberal and Social Democratic parties, led to the "Great Compromise" of 1907–

[8] Differences in the composition of the two houses arose from differences in their electoral base. Deputies to the upper chamber were elected by provincial and city assemblies, while members of the lower house were chosen directly in "popular" elections. Because the right of suffrage was based on taxable wealth, however, the lower middle and working classes were disenfranchised. As a result virtually four fifths of the adult population were ineligible to vote. See Rustow, *Politics of Compromise*, pp. 18–23.

[9] Douglas Verney, *Parliamentary Reform in Sweden, 1866–1921* (Oxford: Clarendon Press, 1957), p. 230.

1909 that provided for universal manhood suffrage in elections to the lower house of parliament and proportional representation in elections to both chambers.[10] The final triumph of democracy was then realized under a Liberal-Social Democratic coalition government in 1918. In the face of threatened disturbances at home and the November revolution in Germany, which led to the abdication of the Kaiser and the proclamation of the Weimar Republic, Sweden's Conservatives concurred with the Liberals and Socialists in introducing universal suffrage. The reform was formally ratified by successive constitutional amendments in 1919 and 1921.

Parallel with the extension of suffrage rights, the principle of parliamentary responsibility became firmly established as the basis of Swedish government. Throughout the nineteenth century "successive constitutional amendments and the slow accretion of custom . . ." had gradually modified the original constitutional separation of powers between the king and parliament.[11] Several categories of law were transferred from royal to joint legislation, while the Riksdag—through its control of state finances—came to exercise greater authority in supervising administrative functions.

Concomitantly the national cabinet, which was originally a group of royal advisers who served at the pleasure of the monarch, assumed a corporate personality of its own. Its members were still responsible to the king rather than to parliament, but in practice the cabinet displaced the monarch as the central focus of executive decisions. The final shift to parliamentary government occurred in 1917 when the Liberals and the Social Democrats formed a coalition ministry with majority support in the lower house. Henceforth the king's choice of prime minister was limited by party alignments in the Riksdag.

In attaining universal suffrage and parliamentarism, Sweden was following precedents that had already been established elsewhere in Scandinavia. Ministerial responsibility was introduced in 1884 in Norway and in 1901 in Denmark. Finland was the first Nordic country to achieve universal suffrage—in 1906—and was followed by Norway in 1913 and Denmark in 1915. Parliamentarism was firmly instituted in Finland when the Finns declared their independence from the new Bolshevik regime in Russia in December 1917.

---

[10] In exchange for agreement on these reforms, the Liberals and Socialists concurred with the Conservative demand to retain the upper house.

[11] Rustow, *Politics of Compromise*, p. 174.

ECONOMIC MODERNIZATION

Accompanying the transformation of the political system was Sweden's industrialization.[12] Like Norway but unlike Denmark and the continental European countries, Sweden never experienced serfdom during the medieval period. Since the consolidation of the early Swedish kingdom, most Swedes had retained an independent existence as small farmers and rural craftsmen. The coastal urban centers of Stockholm, Göteborg, and Malmö were little more than overgrown villages, while industry was limited largely to iron and timber production in the northern provinces.

The predominantly agrarian society of early nineteenth-century Sweden was characterized by economic and social immobility. More than 90 percent of the population lived on farms or in small rural communities, and stringent government controls on trade restricted the expansion of existing industries. Increased competition and new smelting processes abroad contributed further to the stagnation of the production of iron—the nation's principal export.

Commencing with the breakup of the open field system, the abolition of guilds in 1846, and the subsequent advent of free trade, the Swedish economy entered an initial phase of industrialization in the mid-1850s. Prompted largely by classical liberal economic doctrines imported from England and America, these changes helped rationalize agriculture and industrial production and stimulated investments in new technology and factories. Crucial sources of capital were made available for industrialization through the reorganization of the national Riksbank in 1834, the establishment of private banks in 1856, and the influx of credit from Germany and the United States.

Of particular significance for the accelerating pace of industrialization was the creation of a national railway system. Begun under state auspices in the 1850s, Sweden's railway network grew from 527 kilometers in 1860 to 5876 in 1880. By facilitating the rapid transport of agricultural products, iron, and timber, the railways ended the historic isolation of the Swedish countryside and overcame earlier restrictions imposed by distance and terrain on the movement of exports to the coast.

After the rapid economic expansion from the mid-1850s

[12] For more comprehensive treatments of Sweden's economic modernization see Eli F. Heckscher, *An Economic History of Sweden* (Cambridge, Mass.: Harvard University Press, 1954) and G. A. Montgomery, *The Rise of Modern Industry in Sweden* (London: P. S. King and Son, 1939).

through the 1860s followed a period of less dramatic growth. Recurrent agricultural crises, wage fluctuations in industry, and an expanding population generated the first pressures of management-labor conflict and precipitated successive waves of emigration abroad. By the end of the century over a million Swedes had left the country, most of them settling in the United States. In the latter part of the decade a severe recession—initiated by a temporary decline in exports to Germany—provoked demands among farmers and businessmen in favor of tariff protection against foreign competition. Support for more restrictive trade measures grew in parliament where protectionists managed to secure majority approval of higher tariffs and duties in 1887.

Partially as a result of the protectionist victory the Swedish economy entered a stage of rapid and sustained industrial advance in the mid-1890s. New industries such as paper and leather helped counterbalance the earlier decline in the established export sectors, while increased demand for Swedish iron and timber on the continent provided a further impetus for industrial expansion. As the capacity of industry to absorb unskilled workers increased, the persistent agricultural crises were largely overcome.

Table 1   Transformation of Swedish Economy, 1870–1920[a]
Workers in principal occupation categories
(Numbers in millions)

Year	Total Population	Agriculture		Industry and Handicrafts	
		Number	Percent	Number	Percent
1870	4169	3017	72.4	610	14.6
1900	5136	2828	55.1	1426	27.8
1910	5552	2697	48.8	1766	32.0
1920	5905	2596	44.0	2066	35.0

Year	Total Population	Commerce and Transportation		Services and Free Professions	
		Number	Percent	Number	Percent
1870	4169	217	5.2	325	7.8
1900	5136	535	10.4	347	6.7
1910	5552	741	13.4	318	5.8
1920	5905	898	15.2	344	5.8

[a]Adapted from Elis Håstad, *Sveriges historia under 1900-talet* (Stockholm: Bonniers, 1958), p. 71. Population totals from Sweden, Statistiska centralbyrån, *Statistisk årsbok för Sverige 1968* (Stockholm: Statistiska centralbyrån, 1968), p. 28.

By the end of World War I industrialization had fundamentally transformed the basis of the Swedish economy. Within five decades, as Table 1 indicates, the percentate of the nation's population engaged in agriculture had declined from 72 percent to 44 percent. The number of persons engaged in manufacturing and commerce had grown from approximately 20 percent in 1870 to over 50 percent in 1920.

By initiating demographic change and creating new occupational strata, industrialization played a significant role in Sweden's social and political modernization. Important manifestations of the former included urbanization, educational reform, the emancipation of women, and the growth of various popular movements. Social change contributed in turn to the rise of new political parties that constituted the principal forces in Sweden's transition to parliamentary democracy and the subsequent creation of the welfare state.

SOCIAL MODERNIZATION

Defined as the mobilization of social resources on behalf of system transformation, social modernization embraced multiple facets. One aspect was the incipient growth of urban areas. The number of towns increased from 86 in 1800 to 97 in 1914, with the percentage of urban population rising from less than 10 percent to more than 20 percent. Total population more than doubled during the nineteenth century, expanding from 2,347,303 to 5,136,441 by 1900. As tens of thousands Swedes migrated from the countryside to urban districts, they found that the values appropriate to an agrarian society were no longer wholly relevant. Through concentration of numbers and group interaction, new forms of social consciousness emerged that were receptive to organized efforts to achieve sociopolitical reform.

Contributing to the development of attitudes conducive to social modernization were the diffusion of knowledge and attainment of technical skills among an increasing percentage of the population. Traditionally local church parishes had been responsible for primary education in Sweden. The absence of a formal education system meant that in practice a majority of citizens acquired at best a rudimentary knowledge of reading and writing. Only members of the upper socioeconomic strata could afford to send their children to private schools and the universities for advanced studies.[13] Emulating liberal-inspired educational reforms introduced several decades earlier in Denmark and Norway, the Swedish government established a nation-wide elementary school system in 1842.[14] All school-aged children were required to attend a six-year primary school (*folkskola*) for basic courses in language, history, and mathematics. Beyond that level qualified and financially able students could advance to a three-year intermediate school (*realskola*) and a four-year gymnasium. Completion of a comprehensive examination—the *studentexamen* which was equivalent to the *Abitur* in Germany and the *baccalaureate* in France—was the necessary qualification for admission to a university.

The act of 1842 did not overcome inequities in educational opportunity, but it did provide a firm basis for mass literacy and individual mobility in the industrial era. Supplementary efforts were undertaken on private initiative in the 1860s when folk high schools were founded throughout the country. Modelled after the Danish popular education experiment in the 1830s, the folk high schools offered elementary and vocational training to adults. Most were located in rural districts—for the benefit of the agrarian population—and were operated as boarding schools during the winter months.[15]

A third measure of the gathering momentum of social modernization was the gradual modification in the status of women in Swedish society. Throughout the centuries of agricultural predominance, Sten Carlsson observes, "the married woman was as a rule her husband's work comrade."[16] A majority of women were engaged in agrarian pursuits, either on a part-time basis as housewives or full-time as minors or spinsters. Subordinate both legally and socially to men, women possessed few rights of their own. They could not sell or buy property without the permission of their husbands or guardians; they were poorly educated; and they

[13] At the beginning of the nineteenth century there were two universities in Sweden: Uppsala, founded in 1477, and Lund, established in 1668. The universities of Stockholm and Göteborg were founded in 1878 and 1891, respectively, as private colleges.

[14] Compulsory primary education was enacted in 1814 in Denmark and in 1827 in Norway.

[15] Anna-Lisa Kälvesten, *The Social Structure of Sweden* (Stockholm: The Swedish Institute, 1965), p. 61.

[16] Sten Carlsson, "Den sociala omgrupperingen i Sverige efter 1866," in Arthur Thomson (ed.), *Samhälle och riksdag*, II (Stockholm: Almqvist & Wiksell, 1966), p. 298.

could be heavily fined if found guilty of adultery. Only in response to the infusion of liberal thought were women accorded greater equality. They were admitted to public schools under the educational reform act of 1842, acquired equal rights of inheritance in 1845, and were permitted to attend universities in 1873. The following year legislation was passed granting women equal property rights.

With urbanization and industrialization, women began to organize to promote the further liberalization of existing laws and to enter nonagrarian occupations. The Society for Married Women's Rights was formed in 1873, and the Fredrika Bremer Association, which was named after an early advocate of women's emancipation, was established in 1884. The latter was founded "on a program of equal legal, civic, economic, and political status for women."[17] Partly as a result of public agitation by such groups, divorce laws were liberalized in 1915 to permit couples to obtain a divorce by mutual consent and universal suffrage was implemented in the constitutional reform of 1919–1921. With respect to employment, an increasing number of women began to pursue careers previously closed to them—particularly in industry and white-collar professions. By 1920 the percentage of women employed on a full-time basis in agriculture had declined to 14.0 (compared to 21.4 percent in 1870), while the percentages of industrial and salaried women employees increased to 5.2 and 5.6, respectively.[18] In 1923 a new career opportunity became open when women were permitted to enter the civil service.

Politically the most important expression of social modernization was the proliferation of mass-based popular movements during the latter half of the nineteenth century. The leading groups included dissenting religious sects (such as Methodists and Baptists who eventually broke with the established state church), temperance societies, local consumer cooperatives, unions, and new political parties. A related phenomenon was the formation of student clubs—the Verdandi Club in Uppsala and Heimdal in Lund—to further religious and political freedom. Although the specific goals of the various popular associations differed, they served in common as structures of social reintegration for the new industrial-urban population. Among them organized labor and the strictly political associations played the decisive role in Sweden's sociopolitical transformation.

17 Kälvesten, p. 25.
18 Carlsson, p. 301.

EMERGENCE OF A MULTIPARTY SYSTEM

Until economic and social modernization yielded spatial mobility and new forms of group consciousness, little basis existed for joint political action in Sweden. Within the Riksdag representatives of agrarian interests had formed the Ruralist party (*Lantmannapartiet*) in 1867 in opposition to the dominance of the upper house, but they perceived no need to institutionalize a formal party organization outside parliament. Suffrage rights were sufficiently limited so that organized electoral campaigns were not warranted.

Among the population at large workers were scattered in isolated communities and had only limited opportunity for communication or group contact. During the preindustrial phase of agricultural supremacy and guild dominance, paternalistic bonds between employers and laborers effectively precluded the latter's organization. If workers were discontented, they were much more likely to join a temperance or religious society than to form an association of their own.

With the advent of industrialization, the position of workers began to change. The expansion of the timber industry, for example, generated new proletarian groups that were not constrained by the legacy of traditional guild ties among craftsmen and ironworkers. It is hardly surprising, therefore, that Sweden's first large-scale strike occurred in the timber producing district of Sundsvall in 1879. Rootless, massed together, and forced to accept low wages, the strikers proved harbingers of greater militancy among the Swedish working classes.[19]

By the 1880s the widespread adoption of the factory system, the growth of cities and towns, and a rising standard of living had created a propitious environment for organized political reform efforts. In this atmosphere of rapid socioeconomic change arose two major political forces to challenge the established political order: the Social Democratic and Liberal parties.

Socialist thought was introduced in Sweden in the early part of the decade by August Palm, a tailor, who had been inspired by what he had seen of the trade union movement during his travels in Germany and Denmark. In 1881 Palm organized the Swedish

[19] S. M. Lipset notes that, in general, workers in "isolated occupations"—that is, "those occupations which are most isolated, in every sense, from contact with the world outside their own group . . ."—tend to exhibit radical political attitudes. Lipset, p. 104.

Social Democratic Association in Malmö, and founded the nation's first socialist newspaper, *Folkviljan*, a year later. In 1883 he became editor of its successor publication, *Social Democraten*.

An important result of Palm's efforts to propagate socialist ideas throughout the country was a flurry of trade union activity. After 1885 industrial strikes increased in scope and intensity, and, despite employer harrassment in the form of lockouts and dismissals, total trade union membership reached 60,000 by the 1890s.

The free trade controversy of the 1880s cast the extraparliamentary agitation for sociopolitical reform into sharp relief. With the victory of protectionism in 1887 "many who otherwise had no interest in politics and parliamentary affairs [realized] how deeply an Act of Parliament could affect their daily lives, even to the regulation of the price of bread."[20] Awakened to political consciousness and aware of their growing strength through numbers, dissident workers and radical liberal intellectuals began to organize a number of voluntary associations to press their collective demands. Foremost among them was mass agitation on behalf of universal suffrage. With the formation of the Universal Suffrage Association of Sweden in 1890, a national structure was created for the merger of diverse groups espousing electoral reform, religious toleration, and parliamentarism into a unified liberal movement.

In 1889 delegates from over 60 trade unions and Social Democratic clubs convened in Stockholm to found the Swedish Social Democratic party. Although Palm and the early socialist leaders had utilized Marxist parlance to advocate a "new society, a new system, and a new organization of economic life,"[21] members at the congress resolved to cooperate with the nascent liberal movement in a common struggle for suffrage reform. A pivotal figure in the debate on party tactics was Hjalmar Branting. Branting, who had succeeded Palm as editor of *Social Democraten* in 1886, was an outspoken proponent of reformist policies. Several years earlier he had written: "[The] goal of Social Democracy is certainly revolutionary in that it foresees a radical transformation of capitalist society. But the way to this [goal] leads through universal suffrage and . . . peaceful . . . political cooperation."[22]

[20] Verney, p. 108.

[21] Quoted in Herbert Tingsten, *Den svenska socialdemokratiens idéutveckling*, I (Stockholm: Tiden, 1941), p. 81.

[22] Quoted in H. Hilding Nordström, *Sveriges socialdemokratiska arbetareparti under genomsbrottsåren, 1889–1894* (Stockholm: KF, 1938). p. 124.

Together the Social Democratic party and the liberal associations grew in strength during the 1890s. With an increase in party membership to 10,000 by 1895, Branting's election as the first Social Democratic deputy to parliament a year later, and the formation of the national Swedish Federation of Trade Unions (*Landsorganisation*, abbreviated as LO) in 1898, the socialist movement rapidly became an established political force. In 1900, meanwhile, the Liberals formally created their own national party organization, and by 1902 had become the largest party in the lower house of the Riksdag.

Supported by a parliamentary majority the Liberals and the Social Democrats formed a coalition ministry in 1917—with the Liberal chairman, Nils Edén, as prime minister—to establish the principle of cabinet responsibility and introduce universal suffrage. By agreeing to join the Liberals in executive office, the Swedish Socialists thus became "the first party of the Second International to attain cabinet office by legal means and also the first to serve under a crowned head of state."[23]

The rise of the Socialist and Liberal parties meant an irrevocable end to Sweden's traditional political alignments. Following the adoption of manhood suffrage in the constitutional reform of 1907–1909, the once-powerful Ruralist party was decimated in elections to the lower house in 1912. In its place were formed— after several years of flux in names and organization—the lineal ancestors of today's Moderate Unity (Conservative) and Center (Agrarian) parties. The Communists split off from the majority Social Democrats in February 1917 to establish themselves as Sweden's fifth major political party.

SOCIAL DEMOCRATIC ASCENDANCY

The emergence of the Swedish multiparty system as the political expression of underlying socioeconomic and ideological differentiation resembled the concomitant proliferation of parties in other Scandinavian states. By the mid 1920s Norwegian parties included the Communists, Labor, the Left party (which corresponded to the Swedish Liberals), the Agrarians, and the Conservatives. A similar spectrum existed in Denmark except that the Danish Left approximated the Norwegian and Swedish agrarian parties, while liberal forces were organized as the Radical Left.

[23] Rustow, *The Politics of Compromise*, p. 54.

Finland represented a special case in that the party system embraced a sixth political organization, the Swedish People's party, a moderate liberal force representing the linguistic and cultural Swedish minority.

In contrast to parliamentary immobilism throughout much of the continent, where deep ideological and religious cleavages had produced an even greater multiplicity of parties than in Scandinavia, political fragmentation in Sweden did not lead to political instability. At virtually the same time that the Weimar Republic succumbed to the onslaughts of national socialism, Sweden entered a period of orderly socioeconomic and political change that has culminated in today's welfare state. During the critical decades that spanned this process, Sweden—alone among the Nordic states—was spared the debilitating effects of war and occupation.

The Socialist-Liberal coalition of 1917 dissolved in 1920 as a result of party disagreement over social policies. After a desultory phase of minority parliamentarism during the 1920s, in which eight ministries of varying political composition held office because no party could claim a majority in the Riksdag, the Social Democrats assumed cabinet responsibility in 1932 to initiate nearly four decades of virtually uninterrupted one-party dominance of the national executive. The Socialist rise to power was prompted by widespread domestic dissatisfaction over unemployment and falling agricultural prices in the wake of the prevailing international economic crisis. Having increased their share of the popular vote to 41.7 percent in the September 1932 election to the lower house, the Social Democrats formed a government under Per Albin Hansson (who had been elected party chairman after Branting's death in 1926). They consolidated their control of cabinet office when backbench members of the Agrarian party agreed in early 1933 to support the Socialists in exchange for a promise of government subsidies for agriculture. This step marked the beginning of Sweden's present era of majority parliamentarism.

Continued Socialist electoral gains from 1933 to 1939 reflected the apparent success of their expansionist antidepression programs. A minority Agrarian cabinet was appointed during the summer of 1936 when the Socialists resigned after a parliamentary defeat on a pension proposal, but following new elections in September the Social Democrats and Agrarians formalized their earlier tactical alliance in a coalition government. Richard Tomasson suggests that the Agrarians—as a party representing the narrowly defined interests of Swedish farmers—were willing to cooperate with the Socialists "because of [their] lack of commitment on many issues."[24]

In collaboration with the Agrarians, the Socialists embarked on an ambitious social welfare program to implement increased unemployment assistance, childbirth benefits, housing subsidies for large families, vacations for housewives with children, and aid to local communities for the construction of homes for the aged. Legislation was also passed guaranteeing government officials the right to organize, granting industrial workers an annual two-week vacation, and extending the eight-hour working day from industry to agriculture and the retail trades.

In foreign affairs Sweden continued to pursue her traditional policy of neutrality. When war broke out in September 1939, Socialist and Agrarian leaders broadened membership in the coalition government to include the Liberal and Conservative parties. The formation of the wartime coalition provided a necessary concentration of national political forces at a time of Sweden's greatest international peril. After the Soviet Union attacked Finland in 1939 and Germany invaded Denmark and Norway in April 1940, Sweden was isolated for the duration of the European conflict.

As wartime hostilities neared an end in late 1944, internal cabinet cohesion was disrupted when the Social Democrats proclaimed a "27 point program" that called for the socialization of natural resources, selected private firms, and credit institutions in the postwar period.[25] Even though leaders of the Agrarian, Liberal, and Conservative parties favored continued national coalition rule after the cessation of hostilities on the continent, they resolved that they could not endorse the proposed Socialist economic policies. Heightened disagreement within the cabinet culminated in the dissolution of the wartime ministry in July 1945, and Hansson formed a new government composed solely of Social Democrats. When Hansson died in October 1946, Tage Erlander, the 45-year-old Minister of Education and the State Church, became prime minister as the new Social Democratic party leader.

Either alone or as senior partner in a coalition with the Center (Agrarian) Party (1951–1957), the Social Democrats have maintained their control of the national executive throughout the postwar period. By 1972 they had thus established one of the longest records of longevity—40 years in office with only a three

[24] Richard F. Tomasson, *Sweden: Prototype of Modern Society* (New York: Random House, 1970), p. 47.
[25] See Chapter Eight.

month interruption in 1936—of any contemporary ruling party in the democratic political systems of Western Europe, North America, and the British Commonwealth. In Norway and Denmark the Social Democrats have also achieved at least a relative electoral majority, but the strength of nonsocialist forces has prevented them from consistently dominating either government. The Norwegian Labor party was in power from 1935 to 1965, sharing cabinet authority with other parties only during the wartime coalition government in exile in London, but lost to the nonsocialist bloc in the elections of 1965 and 1969. Aggregating an average electoral following of 40 percent during the postwar period, the Social Democrats in Denmark have held office four times since 1945—on three occasions as a minority cabinet and once in coalition with the Radical Left. They were displaced by a nonsocialist coalition in 1968. Because of the greater fragmentation of the party system in Finland, which has precluded a cohesive parliamentary majority, no postwar coalition has exercised cabinet responsibility longer than two years.

SOURCES OF POLITICAL STABILITY

Several factors have combined to reinforce the capacity of the Swedish system to sustain long-term political stability. One is the nature of prevailing elite attitudes. Common political values embracing moderation and a willingness to compromise—products of Sweden's social homogeneity and historical tradition—permeate the nation's political and socioeconomic structures. (These attitudes are explored in greater detail in Chapter Three.) In parliamentary committees as well as Royal Commissions, which are appointed by the cabinet to consider major legislation before it is formally introduced in parliament, party and interest group leaders have repeatedly demonstrated a strong commitment to seeking compromise solutions to controversial measures. That the principal interest associations are accorded considerable autonomy in the labor market and the political process—as indicated in Chapter Six—provides an additional source of stability by relieving the political system of many potential conflicts. Shared values of moderation and pragmatism have not prevented occasionally acrimonious controversies over domestic issues, but they have helped mitigate the divisive effect of party and group cleavage.

Also important is the transformation of the multiparty system. Drawing most of their numerical strength from members of the industrial and agrarian working classes, the Social Democrats have experienced a steady growth in the objective socioeconomic base of their electoral support as the nation has become progressively more industrialized. Because of their ideological moderation they have simultaneously succeeded in extending their appeal to a significant number of middle-class white-collar workers and smaller businessmen. Having displaced the Liberals as the largest party in the lower house as early as 1914, the Socialists have amassed 42 percent or more of the popular vote since 1932.

The persistent majority or near majority status of the Social Democrats during the past four decades has transformed the Swedish multiparty system into a functional bipolar system consisting of the Socialists (tacitly supported on most issues by the Left Party-Communists) and a loosely united nonsocialist bloc. Because the Social Democrats have been able to dominate the national executive in much the same way as a majority party in a two-party system like that in Britain, Sweden has escaped much of the chronic government instability generally associated with multiparty systems elsewhere.

THE MODERN INDUSTRIAL-WELFARE STATE

Under conditions of sustained stability provided by consensual norms among the nation's elites and an entrenched Socialist majority in parliament, the Swedish system has attained its present levels of economic, social, and political modernity. By 1965 the percentage of persons engaged in industry and construction had increased to 44 percent, while that of those in commerce and transportation had risen to 22 percent. Persons employed in services and the free professions totaled 22 percent. The agrarian sector of the economy had declined to 12 percent.

Industrialization has produced an urbanized, affluent, and socially mobile society. In 1965 the number of towns had grown to 132, with 77.4 percent of the population living in urban areas. Sweden's gross national product of $26,250 million (1968) is double that of Denmark and nearly three times as high as Norway's GNP.[26] Earning over $4200 a year (1968), the average Swedish industrial worker receives the highest median income in Europe. In comparison British employees earn approximately $3330, West Germans $2900, and French workers $2000.[27] Continued social modernization is evidenced by greater occupa-

[26] Denmark's GNP was $12.4 billion in 1968 and Norway's was $9.0 billion.
[27] International Labor Organization, *I.L.O. Yearbook of Labor Statistics* (Geneva: International Labor Organization, 1969).

tional mobility among women and a burgeoning student population. By 1940 the percentage of women in white-collar professions had risen to 10.0—displacing agriculture as the largest career category—and reached 17.9 by the beginning of the 1960s.[28] The number of secondary school students increased from 20,100 in 1950 to 115,399 in 1967, while university enrollment grew from 14,300 in 1945 to 98,367 in 1967. To help meet demands for improved education facilities, parliament endorsed legislation in 1950 and 1962 to merge elementary and intermediate schools and create a unitary secondary school system. At the same time a fifth university was established at Umeå in Norrland province.

Important manifestations of political modernity are progressive increments in the rate of political participation and the scope of government sponsored welfare services. From 54 percent of the population who voted in the first election after the adoption of universal suffrage in 1919–1921, political participation has climbed to a postwar average of 81 percent. Social homogeneity and consensual political norms have encouraged the channeling of participation almost exclusively through established socioeconomic organizations and the existing multiparty system. Even at the height of success of right-wing totalitarian movements in the 1930s and 1940s on the continent, no comparable groups managed to secure parliamentary representation in Sweden.[29] In the postwar period the newly founded Christian Democratic Union (KDS)—a popularist party with strong traditional religious overtones—has failed to receive more than 1.5 percent of the national vote. To be sure factionalism is a recurrent marginal feature of modern Swedish politics, but it has been largely confined to new groups within or among the five principal parties.

In the realm of welfare policies, the government has expanded the programs initiated in the late 1930s to include annual children's allowances of nearly $200 per child; free medical insurance in case of accidents or illness; free maternity benefits; housing subsidies; and supplementary pension payments amounting to 60 percent of a person's annual income during the 15 most productive years of his life. In 1965 the Swedish government spent nearly three billion dollars on these and other welfare services—fully 16.9 percent of the national income for an average of $370

---

[28] Carlsson, p. 301.

[29] National extremist movements were formed during the 1930s but never received more than .7 percent of the popular vote. See Rustow, "Scandinavia: Working Multiparty Systems," p. 184.

per citizen.[30] (Comparative data on government sponsored services in Sweden and other advanced nations are presented in Chapter Eleven.) To finance these and other government services, the Swedes pay among the highest taxes in the world. In 1968, their disposable income after taxes as a percentage of personal income was 68 percent, compared to 80 percent in the United States, 81 percent in Britain, and 78 percent in West Germany.[31]

A corollary to the expansion of the welfare state is a significant growth in the size of the government bureaucracy. At the turn of the century only a dozen public administrative agencies existed; by 1960 there were over 40.[32] Concurrently the number of civil servants increased from 44,488 to 301,717.[33]

The twin processes of economic and sociopolitical transformation have thus generated unprecedented capacities for controlling both collective and individual environments in contemporary Sweden. In this respect Sweden is a thoroughly modernized system. Yet the very attainment of modernizing goals has led in Sweden—as it has in the United States, Germany, France, and other advanced systems—to new manifestations of change. Mass affluence, bureaucratization, and the international diffusion of new forms of critical consciousness have created the conditions for Sweden's transition to the postwelfare state.

[30] *Yearbook of Nordic Statistics,* pp. 142–143.

[31] United Nations, *United Nations Yearbook of National Accounts Statistics, 1969, II, International Tables* (New York: United Nations, 1969).

[32] Elis Håstad, *Sveriges historia under 1900-talet* (Stockholm: Bonniers, 1958), p. 151.

[33] Carlsson, pp. 172–173.

TWO
THE COOPERATIVE INDIVIDUALIST
Political socialization, participation, and leadership recruitment

The internal isolation of preindustrial Swedish society has exerted an enduring effect on contemporary behavior. Distance, extensive stretches of forest, and Sweden's intricate maze of lakes and waterways constituted historical barriers to travel and communication. Solitude born of nature's omnipotence helped nurture in the people an introspective individualism and pride in personal achievement. At the same time the common challenge to survival posed by climate and terrain encouraged strong bonds of kinship among families and communities. Hence the Swedes also acquired a sense of collective identity that found expression in group loyalty and a willingness to cooperate with others. Modernization ended the nation's traditional isolation and has drastically altered the material conditions of the Swedes' existence. Yet individualism and group consciousness persist as distinctive attributes of Swedish character in the industrial-welfare state.

Industrialization transformed and strengthened group loyalties in the form of new associations to promote collective goals. With the proliferation of numerous vocational and voluntary groups that accompanied modernization, Sweden acquired its present reputation as a "land of organization."[1] Group conscious-

---

[1] Gunnar Heckscher, *Staten och organisationerna*, 2d ed. (Stockholm: KF, 1951). Also cited in Dankwart A. Rustow, *Politics of Compromise* (Princeton, N.J.: Princeton University Press, 1955), pp. 7 and 46.

ness is highly structured in agricultural and consumer cooperatives, trade unions, employer associations, political parties, and promotional movements such as the various temperance leagues.

Actively committed to an ethic of collective responsibility through membership in multifarious socioeconomic organizations, most Swedes simultaneously retain an intense awareness of self. "The Swedish character, after all, was formed in the country, . . ." Paul Austin notes. "Half a century ago, almost the entire nation lived in [agrarian villages]. Now two-thirds have suddenly moved into town. They have brought with them, one feels, their isolation. Distances, more physical, have become introjected, swallowed. Loneliness has become spiritual."[2]

In interpersonal relations the Swedes' self-awareness is manifest in emotional detachment and social restraint. "There is general agreement on the Swedes," Tomasson writes, "as stolid and stiff, shy or reserved, formal and conventional, inhibited—even dull, nonexpressive, more interested in things than in people, and so forth."[3] And as Prime Minister Olof Palme told David Frost in an interview on BBC: "We're probably shy and reserved, and you once said the humor of hell would have the humor of Sweden. We are distant and perhaps rather dull."[4] Even a casual visit to Sweden will seem to confirm such impressionistic descriptions. The contrast between public decorum in Sweden and the pulsating rhythm of life in other countries, especially in southern Europe, is striking. On the streets, in restaurants, and in public conveyances, most Swedes withdraw into quiet anonymity. "Stockholm," a Swedish journalist once remarked privately, "is a bureaucrat's city —well-organized, efficient, and deadly boring."

The inability of many individuals to establish meaningful contacts with others is a recurrent theme of Swedish literature and films. A modern illustration is the fate of Professor Isak Borg in Ingmar Bergman's film, *Wild Strawberries*. During a dreamlike sequence in which he relives experiences of his youth, Borg witnesses an exchange between his deceased wife and her lover. When the scene has faded he turns to his companion, Alman:

ISAK: Where is she?
ALMAN: You know. She is gone. Everyone is gone. Can't you hear

[2] Paul Britten Austin, *On Being Swedish* (Coral Gables, Fla.: University of Miami Press. 1968), pp. 58–59.
[3] Richard F. Tomasson, *Sweden: Prototype of Modern Society* (New York: Random House, 1970), p. 173.
[4] "Frost vs Palme," *Sweden Now*, 3 (June 1969), 5.

how quiet it is? Everything has beeen dissected, Professor Borg.
A surgical masterpiece. There is no pain, no bleeding, no quivering.
ISAK: It is rather quiet.
ALMAN: A perfect achievement of its kind, Professor.
ISAK: And what is the penalty?
ALMAN: Penalty? I don't know. The usual one, I suppose.
ISAK: The usual one?
ALMAN: Of course. Loneliness.
ISAK: Loneliness?
ALMAN: Exactly. *Loneliness*.
ISAK: Is there no grace?
ALMAN: Don't ask me. I don't know anything about such things.[5]

Linguistic conventions reinforce the inhibitions that often
characterize interpersonal relations. Although the intimate *du* is a
readily accepted form of address among relatives, friends, and
occupational associates, the Swedish equivalent (*ni*) to *Sie* in
German or *vous* in French is socially awkward. The reason is that
Swedes have traditionally used formal titles and third person
forms of address in polite discourse. Because *ni* does not express
any certainty of social status, it suggests "overtones of disdain or
at all events of stand-offishness."[6] As a result, encounters among
strangers or casual acquaintances, when titles are unknown and *du*
is inappropriate, are often strained and banal. Prime Minister
Palme has recently attempted to democratize the language by ad-
dressing everyone as *du*, but the effect remains inconclusive. For
centuries "[p]easants from Dalarna, drunks and His Majesty the
King [have assumed] the privilege of calling everyone else *du*.
The rest of Swedish society squirms at the thought."[7]

The importance of titles in forms of address reflects another
level of self-awareness in modern Swedish society, namely a "preoccupation with performance and success."[8] Ambitious and per-
fectionist in their work, the Swedes tend to measure self-esteem in
terms of recognized achievement. Accordingly they place extraordinary emphasis on academic performance and occupational
status. While the Germans and the British similarly revere high

[5] From "Wild Strawberries" in *Four Screenplays by Ingmar Bergman*, trans.
by Lars Malmstrom and David Kushner. © 1960 by Ingmar Bergman. Reprinted by
permission of Simon & Schuster. Extract from *Wild Strawberries* by Ingmar Bergman. Classic Film script series. Copyright © 1960 by Ingmar Bergman. Lorrimer
Publishing Ltd., London.

[6] Austin, p. 8.

[7] Austin. p. 8.

[8] Herbert Hendin. *Suicide and Scandinavia* (New York: Grune and Stratton,
Inc., 1964). p. 44.

academic or social rank, the Swedes' pervasive reliance on titles to define their identity is distinctive.[9] Herbert Hendin attributes this characteristic to the effect of child rearing practices in Sweden. Whereas Danish mothers foster feelings of dependency among their children by smothering them with affection, Swedish mothers tend to encourage early separation between their children and themselves. Hendin suggests as the explanation for this pattern that the "woman does not like to take care of her child and she prefers to go back to work."[10] Accordingly the Swedish mother "is pleased when she observes evidence of the child's self-sufficiency and independence."[11] In turn children learn "to consider dependency needs unacceptable."[12] Having been taught from early childhood to suppress overt displays of emotion, most Swedes seek in their "[w]ork and performance . . . a major outlet for self-assertion and the discharge of aggression."[13]

In direct antithesis to the inhibiting effects of individual introspection on social mores is the extreme desire for privacy in leisure time pursuits. As if to escape the pressures of conformity and restraint in their social lives, many Swedes retreat on weekends and during their summer vacations into secluded countryside or shoreline existences. There, in a primitive *stuga* (cabin) or

---

[9] Listings of surnames in telephone directories, for example, are alphabeticized according to occupation rather than forenames.

[10] Hendin, p. 50.

[11] Hendin, p. 50.

[12] Hendin, p. 50. Although Hendin's analysis of contemporary "psychosocial" character in contemporary Scandinavia appears clinically accurate, it omits the historical influence of agrarian isolation on patterns of interpersonal relations. Only in the twentieth century have significant numbers of Swedish women pursued vocational careers; hence their encouragement of self-reliance among children has deeper roots than simply their desire to return to work. Hendin concedes himself that widespread female employment is an effect rather than cause of early separation.

[13] Hendin, p. 48. Hendin presents a convincing argument that the opposing patterns of child rearing in Denmark and Sweden, respectively, help explain the relatively high rate of suicide in both countries. (The rate is approximately 20 per 100,000 inhabitants.) Loss of a love object in Denmark will yield ego deprivation and hence a disposition to commit suicide, just as failure to perform according to internalized standards of vocational achievement will lead to the same pathological behavior in Sweden. In Norway, where Hendin maintains that child rearing practices produce a healthier balance between dependency needs and achievement norms, the suicide rate is only 11.8 per 100,000 population. In the case of none of the three Scandinavian countries does Hendin find a correlation between welfare services and suicide, as many Western critics of the welfare state have alleged. Ruth Link notes that suicide rates in the Nordic states are about the same as they were at the turn of the century; moreover, they are exceeded by those of West Berlin, Hungary, Austria, Czechoslavakia, and West Germany. Ruth Link, "Suicide: The Deadly Game," *Sweden Now*, 3–4 (December 1969–January 1970), 40–46.

boat, the Swede seeks contentment in a mystical communion with nature. When alone in natural surroundings, Austin observes, the Swede appears to recover "the integrity of which Society is always threatening him."[14] Austin continues:

> It may seem odd that a folk who so narrowly circumscribe their life-style should have so passionate a notion of it. Yet freedom is paradoxically the most precious of Swedish values. Describing the Swede as a socialist *par excellence* (and in the spiritual, not merely the economic sense), it must also be added in the same breath: he is in no small degree an anarchist. "A Swede's conception of justice," barks Sundbärg, "is that it's intolerable he may not do exactly as he likes."[15]

The Swede thus emerges as a cooperative individualist, one who is highly conscious of self but establishes his identity primarily according to collective norms. In their private thoughts many Swedes may lead a lonely existence, sensitive to the opinion of others yet often unable to establish close personal contacts with them. For these very reasons most tend outwardly to be conformists in their social behavior and to seek perfection in their occupations. Of course, there are many exceptions. In an economy dominated by mass-produced consumer goods and corporate giants such as Volvo, artisans maintain a tradition of individual craftsmanship—ranging from woodcarving and ceramics to exquisite handmade silver and gold products—that finds few parallels in modern nations outside Scandinavia. Numerous dissenting religious sects, small in membership but socially influential, provide an additional measure of noncomformity. Individualism has also animated much of the radical cultural-moral debate that is discussed in the following chapter.

Like Charles Reich's assessment of the dichotomy between the public and private lives of persons who embody the consciousness (Consciousness II) of the modern corporate state, therefore, the Swede maintains a dual character: "The individual has two roles, two lives, two masks, two sets of values. It cannot be said, as is true of the hypocrite, that one set is real and the other false. These two values simply coexist; they are part of the basic definition of 'reality.' "[16]

Politically most Swedes resolve the tension between individ-

---

[14] Austin, p. 96.
[15] Austin, p. 98.
[16] Charles Reich, *The Greening of America* (New York: Random House, 1970), p. 78.

ual and collective consciousness in favor of group solidarity. Processes of political socialization yield common values that transcend particular interests; simultaneously the socializing influences of family, social class, and occupation have produced well-defined group identities that determine the distribution of partisan political attitudes and prevailing patterns of electoral participation.

POLITICAL SOCIALIZATION: AGENTS
OF CULTURAL TRANSMISSION

As Richard Dawson and Kenneth Prewitt have defined the concept, political socialization involves the acquisition of values, beliefs, and knowledge about the political system on both the community and the individual levels. The former level involves "cultural transmission," or the introduction of "new generations into established patterns of thought and action."[17] The latter encompasses "the processes through which a citizen acquires his own view of the political world."[18] Political socialization is thus a *learning* experience in which a person internalizes a general set of values and beliefs as well as a particular self-image of his own political role.

Among the principal agents of political socialization, the family has traditionally played a central role in the cultural transmission of values. Childhood experiences are important for learning basic "impressions of what life really is, how to behave in interpersonal relations, what to expect of others, and what others may demand of you."[19] Change in the content of these early lessons in citizenship has occurred as both the structure of parental authority and the relation of the family to other social organizations have undergone transformation. In preindustrial Sweden the family was the basic unit of social organization. Its structure was patriarchal and authoritarian, and children were taught to "perceive social relations between adult and children as a power-relation clearly defined in terms of dominance and submission."[20] Hal Koch observes: "Children were more often taught to obey

[17] Richard Dawson and Kenneth Prewitt, *Political Socialization* (Boston: Little, Brown and Company, 1969), p. 13.

[18] Dawson and Prewitt, p. 6.

[19] Hal Koch, "The Education of Youth," in J. A. Lauwerys (ed.), *Scandinavian Democracy* (Copenhagen: The Danish Institute, the Norwegian Office of Cultural Relations, and the Swedish Institute in cooperation with the American-Scandinavian Foundation, 1958), p. 283.

[20] Joachim Israel, "Personality Change in a Socially Disturbed Rural Community," *International Social Science Bulletin*, 7 (1955), 19.

than to make decisions themselves; that they should adopt the standards of the older generation was regarded as a matter of course. Resistance was masked by a show of compliance; concealment and pretense erected an insurmountable barrier between children and parents, while giving the false impression that all was as it should be."[21]

With the advent of modernization, increased social mobility has gradually eroded traditional patterns of authority relations within the family. Patriarchal dominance declined as women began to join the labor market, thereby enhancing the independence of women as well as necessitating more active participation by men in child rearing and household duties. Accordingly authority relations in the family have been partially "democratized," with parental emphasis on self-sufficiency among children encouraging norms of independence from early childhood. These tendencies are more pronounced among urban middle-class strata than in working-class families; in the latter case Swedish sociologists have discerned continuing vestiges of authoritarian attitudes among parents toward child rearing.[22]

Modernizing change has also extended the socializing influence of other social organizations, particularly the school. Following the introduction of compulsory primary education in the mid-nineteenth century, public schools have progressively become "the most influential and formative factor [next to the home] in the life of the individual."[23] In 1960 all Swedish children acquired a minimum elementary education of seven years, with approximately 16 percent going on to intermediate and/or secondary schools. The educational reforms of the 1950s and 1960s, which resulted in the introduction of a new nine-year comprehensive school, mean that school will play an even more important role in

---

[21] Koch, p. 283.

[22] Israel offers as an explanation of class differences in parental attitudes toward authority

> "that there exists in many industrial enterprises an authoritarian organization structure, 'a long, narrow hierarchy,' as it has been called. The worker, being in the lowest position in such an hierarchy and exposed to social pressures from above, will in the long run acquire certain values, e.g. a value which may be expressed in the opinion that all interpersonal relations are power relations. . . . The more he has accepted such values, the more he will tend to transfer them to other situations. Therefore, they may guide his behavior at home in the family and, in particular, his conduct toward his children and his attitudes toward their upbringing."

Israel, p. 15.

[23] Koch, p. 285.

a child's early socializing experiences in the future. By the year 2000 Swedish authorities estimate that fully half of the school-age population will complete at least an intermediate-level education. An additional 20 percent are expected to finish 10 to 12 years in school, and 10 percent will continue through 13 or more years.[24]

The emancipation of women and the expansion of welfare services have augmented the significance of extra-familial socializing influences even during preschool years. In 1966 accommodations existed for over 73,000 children of working mothers in daycare centers, while nurseries provided space for an additional 13,400. State supported homes, which numbered 227 in 1966, housed almost 4000 infants; so-called reception homes cared for another 2300.[25]

Concomitantly, the secularization of modern Swedish society has diminished the overt socializing role of the church as a third agent of cultural transmission. Once exercising the primary responsibility for local affairs (including education), the state Lutheran church lost much of its secular power to new communal structures in 1842.[26] Protestant religious doctrines stressing the obligation of citizens to obey established political authority were openly challenged in the latter part of the century by the proliferation of dissenting sects. In subsequent decades the importance of organized religion in the daily lives of citizens perceptibly declined. In contrast to the preindustrial norm of regular attendance in parish churches, few contemporary Swedes take part in religious services—even though 90 percent of the population are nominal members of the state church. Austin reports that a 1966 survey of religious attitudes in a Stockholm suburb revealed that nearly 60 percent of the respondents had not gone to church in years and only 14 percent professed belief in specific Christian doctrines.[27] Religious *values*, on the other hand, continue to permeate Swedish society in the form of secularized moral tenets of radical reform, which are discussed in the following section.

Modernization has therefore occasioned a shift in the relative importance of early socializing influences in Sweden. Organized religion has lost much of its earlier significance as a source of community values, while school and a growing network of other

---

[24] *Education in Sweden* (Stockholm: The Swedish Institute, 1968), p. 1.

[25] Sweden, Statistiska centralbyrån, *Statistisk årsbok för Sverige*, 55 (Stockholm: Statistiska centralbyrån, 1968), pp. 268–269. Hereafter referred to as *Statistisk årsbok 1968*.

[26] See Chapter Four.

[27] Austin, pp. 169–170.

social organizations have partially displaced the traditional primacy of the family. Nevertheless the family remains the "dominant group for every child (except those who are brought up in other institutions), and the impulses that come from the family belong to the most important in the development of each individual."[28] Early impressions of national identity which are derived from the family and explicit citizenship training functions performed by schools decisively affect the content of the general values and beliefs that distinguish Swedish political culture.

COMMUNITY VALUES AND BELIEFS

Sweden's social and ethnic homogeneity has proved conducive to the emergence of a more cohesive national system of values than is true of many other advanced nations. In the absence of deeply rooted particularist, linguistic, and class cleavages, modernization has resulted in common socialization experiences that yield largely uniform attributes of what Almond and Verba have defined as a "participant political culture." A predominantly participant political culture, in their terms, is "one in which the members of the society tend to be explicitly oriented to the system as a whole and to both the political and administrative structures and processes."[29] No discernible subcultures exhibit "malevolent" attitudes toward political authority—as is the case among many blacks, right extremists, and Appalachian whites in the United States.[30] Nor, except for the migratory Lapps in the north, are there significant numbers of persons with strictly "parochial" orientations; that is, persons who expect "nothing from the political system . . ." or have a "comparative absence of expectations of change initiated by the political system."[31] A minority of citizens manifest "subject" orientations toward the political system, which

[28] Georg Karlsson, "Familjen," in Gösta Carlsson, et al., Svensk samhällsstruktur i sociologisk belysning (Stockholm: Svenska Bokförlaget, 1965), p. 37.

[29] Gabriel Almond and Sidney Verba, The Civic Culture (Boston: Little, Brown and Company, 1965), p. 18.

[30] For a sampling of the literature on malevolent political attitudes in the United States see Edward S. Greenberg, "Children and Government: A Comparison Across Racial Lines," Midwest Journal of Political Science, 14 (May 1970), 249–275; Robert A. Schoenberger, ed., The American Right-Wing: Readings in Political Behavior (New York: Holt, Rinehart and Winston, Inc., 1969); and Dean Jaros, Herbert Hirsch, Frederick J. Fleron, Jr., "The Malevolent Leader: Political Socialization in an American Sub-Culture," American Political Science Review, 62 (June 1968), 564–575.

[31] Almond and Verba, p. 17.

Almond and Verba describe as passive awareness of system performance but with low "orientations toward specifically input objects, and toward the self as an active participant."[32] This is true to the extent that some Swedes fail to vote or have become critically conscious of their relative lack of personal efficacy in the modern corporate state. On the whole, however, Swedish political culture is congruent with opportunities for mass participation in politics and established pluralist structures.

This does not mean that there are no regional or subculture variations in the content of Swedish values. Provincial consciousness pervades rural communities in the central and southern parts of the country, many of whose inhabitants are distrustful of the secularizing tendencies in the dominant urban culture. Regional identity of another sort characterizes the northern provinces, where the physical isolation of mining towns contributes to a sense of sociopolitical separation from the rest of the nation. Religious differences, too, persist, although clearly without the political consequences of strife between Catholics and Protestants on much of the continent, between the "self-conscious Christian minority and the indifferent majority."[33] But these variations are relatively minor in the larger national context of an overwhelmingly urbanized, industrialized, and secularized society.

The community values of modern Swedish political culture encompass national pride, a sense of individual political competence, and a pervasive moral commitment to sociopolitical activism. Shared values of "affection and support for the political system . . ."[34] are engendered through the positive evaluation in families and schools of national achievements such as Sweden's legacy of neutrality and peaceful transition to democracy. Historical isolation and the attainment of an affluent welfare state have given the Swedes "a sense of distinctiveness of their nation and a feeling of pride, bordering on superiority, over national accomplishments."[35] Highly conscious of Sweden's small state status within the international community, the Swedes do not translate such awareness into zealous nationalism. National pride is tempered by a pragmatic perception of the state as a service organization (rather than a mystical entity demanding the subordination of

[32] Almond and Verba, p. 17.
[33] Tomasson, p. 201.
[34] Thomas J. Anton, "Policy-Making and Political Culture in Sweden," *Scandinavian Political Studies*, 4 (New York: Columbia University Press, 1969), p. 95.
[35] Anton, p. 95.

the individual to abstract goals of statescraft) and a collective "outer-directedness" toward other countries. Gustafsson notes: "There are touches of formality, of ambition, of greater seriousness than is actually required in our way of discussing the things with the world around us. There is an ambition to keep up with and not lose track of what is happening outside our boundaries. . . ."[36]

Positive supports for the political system are accompanied by a "high level of citizen awareness and knowledge about government."[37] Most Swedes have television sets in their homes; because of compulsory universal education, virtually all are literate. With a daily circulation of 514 newspapers per 1000 inhabitants, Sweden ranks first in the world in press readership.[38] Anton cites public opinion surveys in 1967 that "revealed that 90 percent of a national sample were able to identify . . . Palme's party allegiance, while 62 percent of the sample correctly identified Sven Wedén as the newly-selected leader of the Liberal Party." Over 90 percent had at least "heard about" the European Economic Community, and more than half could correctly identify it.[39]

The basis for a widely diffused sense of individual political competence is provided by liberalizing trends in family authority relations and formal training to citizenship in schools.[40] (Reinforcing mechanisms of membership in occupational groups and political parties are discussed later.) In the latter case required courses in civics and Swedish history emphasize democratic principles and individual rights, with students encouraged to anticipate active participation in the nation's politics. Generally the pedagogical quality of Swedish citizenship training is high, as many schools are staffed with persons possessing advanced university degrees.

During the postwar period Swedish secondary education has contributed an additional socializing influence on political atti-

[36] Lars Gustafsson, *The Public Dialogue in Sweden* (Stockholm: P. A. Norstedt & Söners Förlag, 1964), p. 7.

[37] Anton, p. 95.

[38] United Nations, *United Nations Statistical Yearbook* (New York: United Nations, 1968), pp. 774–775. Britain is second with a circulation of 488 newspapers per 1000 followed by Japan with 465, West Germany with 328, and the United States with 309.

[39] Anton, p. 95.

[40] James Coleman defines political competence as awareness of "what one's role is or can be in the system." Coleman (ed.), *Education and Political Development* (Princeton, N.J.: Princeton University Press, 1965), p. 18. As used in this chapter, political competence is equated with the attitudinal attributes of a participant political culture.

tudes in the form of new opportunities for direct student participation in politics. As in the United States, contradictions have long existed in Sweden between the ideal of citizenship as it is presented in classroom discussion and the reality of an authoritarian school system. Taught theoretical principles of political democracy in class, students have traditionally been subjected to curriculum requirements and disciplinary norms imposed on them by school administrators and teachers. Jan Myrdal scathingly describes some of the effects of such constraints on his own adolescent experience:

> The spring of 1943 as I was going to Bromma Secondary School. The days were yellow and sticky like old glue. Sour smell of damp cloth. No time to read and no time to study. The school stole all my time. The long school day was a desert of hopelessness. I was fifteen years old and they tried to make me a happy homeworkdoer by saying that I—if I continued to follow the schedule and answer by rote for yet another fifteen or twenty years—with my brains would become a Ph.D. and jump from pupil's desk to professor's chair. Ignorant and inexperienced as I was, I saw no possibility of breaking this vicious circle. I can still wake up at night with a nauseous feeling, dreaming I am back in Bromma Secondary School and have this perspective of damnation ahead of me.[41]

To help overcome the feelings of anomie that many postwar Swedish youth clearly shared with Myrdal, a group of students organized the Swedish Union of Secondary School Students (SECO) in 1952 to present student views on pending educational reform. From an initial membership of 70 students, SECO had grown by 1970 into a national trade union with 34,000 members in 560 schools. Overcoming early resistance among educators in its efforts to promote "school democracy," SECO won national acclaim by politicians and the press when students assumed direct responsibility for classroom instruction during a national three-week teachers' strike in the fall of 1966.

SECO's demands for greater student influence in public education have already been partially realized in a new experimental school in Stockholm where even first graders "are encouraged to have their say in the whole set-up of instruction and discipline with 'class room councils' that determine the final form and pace

---

[41] Jan Myrdal, *Confessions of a Disloyal European* (New York: Pantheon Books, a division of Random House, Inc., 1968), p. 17.

of education. The teacher guides and co-ordinates, rather than imposing his own ideas, and never assumes authoritative attitudes."[42] One of the instructors has described the school, which SECO endorses as a model for future reform throughout the nation, as follows:

> To be fully effective as the basis for true school democracy, training for such cooperation of teachers and pupils on a near-equal footing must be practised from the earliest stage. If one only starts in the upper age groups, one runs the risk of the elected student councils adopting authoritarian status. We therefore firmly believe in "democracy from scratch" from the first grade onwards.[43]

As only about a third of Sweden's secondary students belong to the union, SECO is not representative of the total school population. Many students remain untouched by its activities, particularly in rural communities, and/or do not accept its policy objectives. Nevertheless SECO has probably strengthened the sense of political competence among younger Swedes, affording an active minority of students the possibility to augment their knowledge of abstract principles of responsible citizenship with practice in participatory rights and obligations.

On the university level extensive opportunities for student participation in politics exist in debating clubs (such as Verdandi in Uppsala) and party student groups. The latter include Social Democratic, Liberal, and Conservative organizations as well as the socialist oriented Clarté Association. In addition all students are required to join the Swedish National Union of Students, which serves as the official spokesman for student views on administrative and educational policies.[44] Only a minority, however, are actively involved in student politics. "Political activity among Swedish young people is enormous but concentrated in a small group . . ." one 21-year-old Swede has said. "For those who are politically active, politics is not a hobby, not a job, but a way of life. Everything is politics. But they are few."[45] Tomasson estimates that at "Uppsala, where student politics are particularly active, not more than 15 percent of the students are members of any political association, including Verdandi."[46] With respect to

---

[42] Michael Salzer, "School Union," *Sweden Now*, 3 (May 1969), 46.
[43] Salzer, pp. 46–47.
[44] Tomasson, pp. 152–153.
[45] Maria-Pia Boëthius, "Politics," *Sweden Now*, 3 (May 1969), 30.
[46] Tomasson, p. 154.

the distribution of political attitudes among university student, one student has said: "Of my generation perhaps 10 percent are revolutionary Marxists, 30 percent are liberals or conservatives, and 60 percent reformist social democrats."[47]

Underlying national pride and individual political competence is a shared tendency among many Swedes to base their sociopolitical behavior on intense moral convictions. Displaying numerous recent manifestations—ranging from the New Left-radical liberal critique of domestic politics and American involvement in Vietnam to the government's postwar policy of international activism[48]—the pervasiveness of moral criteria in evaluative orientations is a product of the nation's religious heritage. Despite the decline of the church as an active agent of socialization, "pietistic or traditional religious values and morals are still widely diffused in Sweden. It is, indeed, striking how many of the leading critics and writers . . . have emerged from the milieu and homes where such beliefs have been strongly represented."[49]

On an individual level, Dag Hammarskjöld expressed a highly personal affirmation of social consciousness rooted implicitly in religious belief when he wrote in his diary:

> Hunger is my native place in the land of the passions. Hunger for fellowship, hunger for righteousness—for a fellowship founded on righteousness, and a righteousness attained in fellowship.
>
> Only life can satisfy the demands of life. And this hunger of mine can be satisfied for the simple reason that the nature of life is such that I can realize my individuality by becoming a bridge for others, a stone in the temple of righteousness.
>
> Don't be afraid of yourself, live your individuality to the full— but for the good of others. Don't copy others in order to buy fellowship, or make convention your law instead of living the righteousness.
>
> To become free and responsible. For this alone was man created, and he who fails to take the Way which could have been his shall be lost eternally.[50]

[47] Paul Britten Austin, "On Not Being Swedish," *Sweden Now*, 4 (October 1970), 27–28.

[48] See Chapters Three and Ten.

[49] Lars Gyllensten, "Swedish Radicalism in the 1960s: An Experiment in Political and Cultural Debate," in Hancock and Sjoberg (eds.), *Politics in the Post-Welfare State: Responses to the New Individualism* (New York: Columbia University Press, 1972).

[50] Dag Hammarskjöld, *Markings*, trans. by Leif Sjöberg and W. H. Auden (New York: Alfred A. Knopf, Inc., 1964), p. 53.

An explicit link between religion and political attitudes exists in the historical alignment between the dissenting Protestant sects and the Liberal party. During the last half of the nineteenth century the free churches emerged as a major focus of liberal opposition to the established oligarchical system. As religious dissenters came to perceive that the attainment of political freedom was a requisite for their avowed goal of religious freedom, many joined the nascent liberal movement. No formal ties were established between the free churches and the Liberals, but the Liberal party continues to recruit many of its adherents among religious dissenters today.

Within the general population religious values have assumed a more indirect influence in the form of the secularized morality of the Social Democratic party and the welfare state. Much of the popular appeal of the early Socialists, particularly among timber and agrarian workers, was rooted in their ideological affinity with Judeo-Christian doctrines of human compassion and justice. In his memoirs Ernst Wigforss, who was widely recognized as the leading socialist intellectual in the mid-twentieth century, attributed part of his decision to embrace socialism to efforts by his contemporaries to translate traditional moral principles into a secular ethic of "welfare morality."[51] A close observer of modern Swedish society has said that the quest for equality in the welfare state "could be taken straight out of Isaiah. Secularized as we are, we have failed to discover that our faith in certain tenets of the Social Democratic party is largely a substitute for religion. And these tenets differ but slightly from those in the Bible."[52]

Within the general framework of these shared community values, the Swedes define their specific political identities in terms of partisan loyalties that are distributed among the five major parties. Two factors "that facilitate the formation of stable partisan alignments in the electorate, . . ." Bo Särlvik observes, are the "parties' anchorage in different social strata as well as the linkages between the party system and a highly developed network of interest organizations presumed to connect perceptions of group interests with party identification in the electorate."[53]

[51] Ernst Wigforss, *Minnen*, I (Stockholm: Tiden, 1950), p. 230.

[52] Private correspondence.

[53] Bo Särlvik, "Party Politics and Electoral Opinion Formation: A Study of Issues in Swedish Politics 1956–1960," *Scandinavian Political Studies*, 2 (New York: Columbia University Press, 1967), p. 173.

OCCUPATION AND CLASS

Socioeconomic differentiation, the growth of new vocational organizations, and the emergence of the contemporary multiparty
system in Sweden occurred simultaneously. As industrial employees, farmers, white-collar workers, businessmen, and industrialists formed more or less inclusive associations to promote their
respective interests, the various strata came to identify their own
group interests with the goals of particular political parties.[54]
Hence occupation, class background, and membership in secondary associations serve as mutually supporting socializing influences in the formation of partisan political allegiances.

Electoral studies have repeatedly demonstrated a correlation
between occupation and party preference.[55] As Table 2 indicates,
three quarters of the industrial workers support the Social Democrats. The second closest coincidence of occupation and partisan
identification is that between the farmers and the Center party (61
percent). Nearly 40 percent of Sweden's industrialists, top businessmen, and higher-level salaried employees endorse the Moderate Unity party, while the Liberals appeal predominantly to
businessmen and white-collar workers.

Occupation, rather than any specific rural-urban cleavage,
also accounts for differences in regional patterns of electoral behavior. Thus agrarian support for the Center party is predictably
concentrated in the farming belt across south-central Sweden,
while the Socialists and the Liberals have traditionally aggregated
most of their followers in mixed rural-urban districts and the
cities. Diverse urban strata provide the principal source of electoral strength for both the Conservatives and the Communists,
although the latter also claim a fairly large following among
miners and industrial workers in the northern mining and timber
provinces. Continuing urbanization has reduced many of the earlier regional variations in party support, with urban elements now
dominating in all five parties.

To the extent that occupation determines, at least in part,

[54] The role of interest groups is explored in Chapter Four.
[55] Incisive recent analyses of Swedish electoral behavior are three articles by
Särlvik: "Political Stability and Change in the Swedish Electorate," *Scandinavian
Political Studies*, I (New York: Columbia University Press, 1966), pp. 188–222;
"Party Politics and Electoral Opinion Formation," pp. 167–202; and "Socio-
economic Determinants of Voting Behavior in the Swedish Electorate," *Com-
parative Political Studies*, 2 (April 1969), 99–135. Earlier studies include Elis
Håstad, *et al., "Gallup" och den svenska väljarkåren* (Stockholm: Hugo Gebers
Förlag, 1950) and Rustow, *Politics of Compromise*, pp. 116–143.

Table 2 Percentage Distribution of Party Preferences within Various Occupational Groups (1968)[a]

Occupational Groups	Party Preference			
	Left Party-Communists	Social Democrats	Center	Liberals
Big businessmen, professionals, and high-level salaried employees	0	14	16	27
Farmers	0	6	61	9
Small businessmen	0	31	24	22
Lower-level salaried employees	1	43	14	24
Agricultural and timber workers	1	56	27	8
Industrial workers	2	75	10	7

Occupational Groups	Party Preference			
	Moderate Unity	Nonsocialist Coalition	Other, NA	Total
Big businessmen, professionals, and high-level salaried employees	39	1	3	100
Farmers	19	0	5	100
Small businessmen	16		7	100
Lower-level salaried employees	15	1	2	100
Agricultural and timber workers	6		2	100
Industrial workers	3	0	3	100

[a]Adapted from Bo Särlvik "Voting Behavior in Shifting Electoral Winds: An Overview of the Swedish Elections 1964–1968, *Scandinavian Political Studies*, 5 (New York: Columbia University Press, 1970), p. 278.

differences in social status among the working, middle, and upper classes, class identification tends to sustain the effect of occupation on partisan electoral choice. In fact, recent studies indicate that class plays a more important role in attitude formation than subsequent occupational mobility. In a study of political influentials in four local communities, for instance, Swedish scholars found that a majority of the members of the lower class (comprising primarily industrial workers) support the Social Democrats, while most upper-class voters (including businessmen, managers, and persons with a university education) endorse the Moderate Unity party and, to a lesser extent, the Liberals. Those within the middle class (for example, white-collar workers and farmers) distribute their support largely between the Liberals and the Center party.[56]

Confirming the effect of class membership on attitude formation in Sweden are studies of income levels and voting behavior. A relative majority of persons earning 9999 crowns or less a year and more than half of those earning between 10,000 and 19,999 crowns sympathize with the Social Democrats. In contrast 53 percent of persons within the highest income level, that is, those receiving 30,000 crowns or more, support the Moderate Unity party. The Liberals attract most of their following among persons earning 20,000 crowns or more. Like the Social Democrats the Center party is predominantly a low-income party, deriving more than half of its electoral support among voters earning less than 10,000 crowns.[57]

The role of social class as a determinant of partisan political alignments is enhanced by family socialization patterns that mitigate the effect of either upward or downward social mobility on party identification. Subjective accounts tend to minimize the role of parental influences in shaping political attitudes in adult life. Nils Edén, the Liberal prime minister of the Liberal-Social Democratic coalition that introduced parliamentarism in 1917, has written of his childhood: "There was little talk concerning national policies or general social problems either at home or among relatives and friends."[58] He describes the milieu of his home life as "so homogeneous that there was hardly any reason to engage in political discussions."[59] Wigforss makes no direct references to his parents' political views, attributing his introduction to socialist thought almost entirely to his experiences as a student in Lund.[60] Yet survey data indicate that the political attitudes of parents do strongly influence those of their children, just as the fact that Eden's social origins were middle class and that Wigforss' father

[56] Bo Anderson, "Opinion Influentials and Political Opinion Formation in Four Swedish Communities," *International Social Science Journal*, 320–336. See also Bo Anderson, "Some Problems of Change in the Swedish Electorate," *Acta Sociologica*, 6 (1962), 241–254.

[57] Sweden, Statistiska centralbyrån, *Riksdagsmannavalen åren 1959–1960*, II (Stockholm: Statistiska centralbyrån, 1961), p. 57. The official exchange rate is 5.165 Swedish crowns to one United States dollar.

[58] Nils Edén, *Minnen* (Stockholm: Albert Bonniers Förlag, 1969), p. 42.

[59] Edén, p. 43.

[60] Wigforss, pp. 131–203.

was a member of the working class presumably predisposed them
to become a Liberal and a Socialist, respectively.

Among sons who were engaged in the same occupation as
their fathers, according to one study, 73.9 percent whose fathers
had favored the Social Democrats also endorsed the Socialists; the
corresponding percentages were 71.1 for Liberal supporters, 57.1
for Center party adherents, and 54.1 for Conservatives. Even
when sons pursue different careers than their fathers, a majority
retain the political views of their fathers (68.1 percent of the
Socialist respondents and 61.4 percent of the Liberals and Conservatives). Only in the case of the Center party was there a
marked generational deviation: 25.4 percent of those who
changed occupations endorsed their fathers' choice of the Center
party, while 23.9 percent switched their political allegiance to the
Social Democrats and 15.5 percent to the Liberals.[61] (The probable explanation for these shifts is that most of the socially mobile
agrarian youth became industrial and white-collar workers and
thus acquired political attitudes that were congruent with their
new socioeconomic status.) In light of similar findings based on a
comparison of political attitudes in a local Swedish community
and among students at Uppsala University, Bo Anderson thus
concludes that "the class of [social] origin makes quite a big
difference. Those among the middle class who come from a working-class background are much more likely to vote Socialist and
much less likely to vote for the Conservative and Liberal parties
than those who come from the middle or upper classes. Also,
working-class people whose parents were middle or upper class
are less likely to be Social Democrats and slightly more likely to
be Conservative or Liberals than other workers."[62] Gunnar
Heckscher interprets such evidence of intergenerational stability
of political attitudes as an expression of class solidarity: "With
the increasingly static character of Swedish life, the concept of
class solidarity has in some respects gained rather than lost in
power over public opinion. In the eyes of many people, even if
you manage to improve your position so as to alter your status, it
is your duty to preserve your allegiance to the class into which you
were born."[63]

The effects of occupation and social class on partisan politi-

[61] Georg Karlsson, "Political Attitudes among Male Swedish Youth," *Acta
Sociologica*, 3 (1958), 233.

[62] Anderson, "Some Problems of Change in the Swedish Electorate," p. 243.

[63] Gunnar Heckscher, "Pluralist Democracy: The Swedish Experience," *Social
Research*, 25 (December 1948), 444.

cal preferences are marginally qualified by differences in sex and marital status. Presumably because fewer women work and hence are subject to the socializing influences of trade unions, women tend to be slightly more conservative in their political orientations than men.[64] Fifty percent of women students from working-class backgrounds who were interviewed in one poll identified with one of the nonsocialist parties, compared to 43 percent of male students with working class origins. A similar tendency was noted in responses by sex to controversial economic issues. Among women with working-class parents 24 percent agreed with recurrent nonsocialist electoral demands for a reduction in taxes; the corresponding percentage for working-class men was 17.[65]

With respect to marital status, 52 percent of married persons who were interviewed during the 1964 electoral campaign favored the Social Democrats; among single men and women the percentage of Socialist support was 47 and 41, respectively.[66] The probable reason for the weaker endorsement of the Social Democratic party among single persons is that they benefit less from Socialist-initiated welfare services. Accordingly they are more likely to respond favorably to intermittent nonsocialist proposals to lower taxes.

POLITICAL PARTICIPATION

Primarily because antecedent political attitudes, derived from family and class backgrounds, are reinforced by an emphasis on group solidarity within the various occupational strata, Sweden manifests high degrees of electoral stability and mass participation in politics. Political landslides are virtually unknown. The greatest postwar electoral shift between the Social Democrats and the nonsocialist bloc occurred in 1966 when Socialist strength declined 5.1 percentage points. Since 1946 fluctuations in popular support between the two blocs have averaged only 2 percent in successive elections.

Testifying to the stability of voting patterns in Sweden is the

[64] That fewer women work is in turn a function of differences in sex roles, with many women discouraged to pursue vocational careers because of their principal responsibility for child rearing and household duties. Variations in the rate of political participation among women and men that derive from differences in sex roles, however, have become largely negligible. See below, p. 56.

[65] Anderson. "Some Problems of Change in the Swedish Electorate," p. 246.

[66] Sweden, Statistiska centralbyrån, *Riksdagsmannavalen åren 1961–1964*, II (Stockholm: Statistiska centralbyrån, 1965), p. 95.

persistence of the electorate's partisan allegiances. An opinion survey in 1960 revealed that 72 percent of the eligible voters remained loyal to the party with which they had identified a week before the election, while only 7 percent were undecided and 6 percent changed their support from one party to another. The percentage of loyal party supporters was highest among Socialist voters. Eighty five percent of those who had sympathized with the Social Democrats actually voted for them in the election. The corresponding percentages for the nonsocialist parties were 81 percent for the Moderate Unity party, 73 percent for the Center party, and 71 percent for the Liberals.[67]

In addition to their strong partisan loyalty, the Swedes are far more active participants in the electoral process than American voters. Since 1948 political participation has averaged 81 percent (compared to 60.5 percent in postwar presidential elections in the United States), reaching a peak of 89.3 percent in 1968. Participation is highest among businessmen and high-level salaried employees and lowest among agrarian, timber, and industrial workers. According to a 1960 survey, participation ranged from approximately 95 percent to about 83 percent for each group, respectively.[68] These variations can probably be attributed to the longer time that members of the upper and middle classes spend in school, which increases their exposure to socializing influences that encourage individual political competence. Differences in sex roles which discouraged participation by women in previous decades have become largely inconsequential in their effect on electoral behavior. For example, 84.8 percent of Swedish women and 86.9 percent of the men voted in the 1964 election.[69]

As a partial explanation of both partisan loyalty and the high rate of electoral participation, Stein Rokkan's observations concerning participatory patterns in Norway would seem to apply equally to Sweden. He writes: "Cross-tabulations against sex, age, education, and socioeconomic position give fairly consistent indications of the importance of *role expectations in every day life*: the more the citizen is expected to deal independently with matters outside his immediate household or his work group, the more he is likely to take an active interest in politics at election time."[70]

---

67 Rune Sjödén, *Sveriges första TV-val* (Stockholm: Sveriges Radio, 1962), pp. 98–100.

68 *Riksdagsmannavalen åren 1959–1960*, p. 56.

69 Elina Haavio-Mannila, "Sex Roles in Politics," *Scandinavian Political Studies*, 5 (New York: Columbia University Press, 1970), p. 213.

70 Stein Rokkan, *Citizens, Elections, Parties* (Oslo: Universitetsforlaget, 1970), p. 355. Italics in the original.

Beyond citizenship training in schools, such role expectations are inculcated in Sweden through the socializing effects of mass membership in occupation related associations and political parties. In his study of patterns of electoral change, Anderson found that workers, who comprise the largest occupational stratum, are subject to multiple pressures to participate in elections through membership in the Swedish Federation of Trade Unions (LO) and various organizations aligned with the Social Democrats such as the party's youth and women's associations.[71] From the moment a young Swede joins a union or a party organization, he encounters intense appeals to group solidarity in partisan publications and electoral manifestos. A major consequence of overlapping membership in occupational and party groups, for workers as well as persons in other socioeconomic strata, is that "participation tends to become cumulative."[72]

The strength of party organization also appears to play a significant role in both the socialization and mobilization of Swedish voters. All five parties have highly institutionalized national and local structures that perform more than simply nomination or campaign functions. "A party in Sweden as elsewhere in Europe," Dankwart Rustow notes, "is not only a political apparatus; it is also a civic club, a pressure group, and an organization for the pursuit of various leisure-time interests."[73] The Social Democrats, in particular, have concentrated much of their efforts on building a strong organization on behalf of long-term party goals. Their emphasis on day-to-day grass root participation is viewed as a "means to enable the organization to achieve far reaching reforms of the entire society along the lines of what was seen as the interest of the working class."[74]

The importance of party organization as a factor encouraging mass political participation in Sweden is reflected in the ratio of party members to voters, which is one of the highest among the Western democracies. (See Table 3.) Nearly half of the Socialist supporters in the 1964 election were members of the Social Democratic party—most of them because of the LO's policy to encourage collective membership of entire unions within the party. The second highest ratio—that for the Moderate Unity Party—

[71] Anderson, "Some Problems of Change in the Swedish Electorate," pp. 248–249.

[72] Anderson, p. 249.

[73] Dankwart A. Rustow, *The Politics of Compromise* (Princeton, N.J.: Princeton University Press, 1955), p. 144.

[74] Anderson, "Some Problems of Change in the Swedish Electorate," p. 249.

Table 3   Percentage of Party Members among Voters[a]

Party	Party Membership (in 1,000s)	Votes (1964)	Percentage of Party Members		
			1964	1948	1932
Left Party-Communits	22,987	221,746	10	29	17
Social Democrats	867,613	1,006,923	43	44	35
Center	116,113	569,934	20	56	17
Liberals	89,489	723,988	11	11	24
Moderate Unity	196,352	582,609	34	28	28
All Parties	1,292,554	4,245,780[b]	34	35	28

[a]Figures for 1964 are calculated from *Statistisk årsbok 1968*, pp. 410 and 417. The data for 1932 and 1948 are from Dankwart A. Rustow, *The Politics of Compromise: A Study of Parties and Cabinet Government in Sweden* (Princeton, N.J.: Princeton University Press, 1955), p. 151.

[b]The total includes votes for a nonsocialist electoral alliance.

equals the national average of one-third party members to voters. Parallel women's and youth associations provide additional sources of party support. The Social Democrats claim the largest organized following among women, while the Center party has the strongest affiliated youth movement. (See Table 4.)

Table 4   Membership in Women and Youth Party Organizations 1964[a]

Party	Women's Organization	Youth Organization
Left Party-Communists		8,000[b]
Social Democrats	66,000	50,000
Center	62,000	80,000
Liberals	15,000	12,000
Moderate Unity	62,000	30,000

[a]Pär-Erik Back, "Det svenska partiväsendet," Arthur Thomson (ed.), *Samhälle och riksdag*, II (Stockholm: Almqvist & Wiksell, 1966), pp. 56–60.

[b]The Communist youth organization is officially independent of the Left Party-Communists.

For a majority of Swedish citizens, then, political participation is a product of complementary processes of childhood and adult socialization experiences. In individual cases sex and marital status exert some influence over electoral behavior, but social background and occupation are the principal determinants of political attitudes and partisan choice. Membership in occupation related associations and, to a lesser extent, political parties strengthens established patterns of political identification by encouraging party loyalty and widespread electoral participation.

LEADERSHIP RECRUITMENT

Interest associations and political parties assume particular significance for those Swedes who are more than nominally involved in the political process. Since the advent of modernization both have served as principal avenues of recruitment for the nation's political leadership. In place of the oligarchic-bureaucratic elite of the nineteenth century has emerged a politically active stratum that is broadly representative of Sweden's major socioeconomic divisions and organized interests.

According to one Swedish survey, a majority of local political influentials are simultaneously active in various interest groups, political parties, and party youth organizations. Ninety-three percent of working class influentials were members of the LO, compared to 81 percent and 64 percent of middle- and upper-class influentials, respectively, who belonged to trade unions or employer associations.[75] On the basis of these findings Anderson concludes that "holding office in one organization increases the possibility that a person later will be elected to another office in *the same or in another organization* . . . . Many people are led into politics in this way because political parties try to recruit individuals who are active and well known in organizations in order to attract the votes of members."[76]

A comparable pattern prevails among national political leaders. All of the contemporary party chairmen advanced to their present leadership positions on the basis of their high status in private organizations or professional party service. Prior to his election as Center chairman, Thörnbjörn Fälldin served as an official in an agrarian youth organization and vice-chairman of the

[75] Anderson, "Opinion Influentials and Political Opinion Formation," p. 325.
[76] Anderson, p. 325.

party. Gösta Bohman, chairman since 1970 of the Moderate Unity party, entered politics after a successful executive career in private business. The leader of the Left Party-Communists, Carl Hermansson, worked his way through the party hierarchy as a journalist and editor in chief of the party's newspaper, *Ny Dag*.

Within the Social Democratic and Liberal parties, apprenticeship in the party youth organizations has proved an important springboard into politics. Sweden's present prime minister, Olof Palme, acquired his early political expertise as a prominent member of the Socialist Youth Association, as did Hansson (prime minister from 1932 to 1946), Gustav Möller (former minister of the social department), and Torsten Nilsson (present foreign minister). The chairman of the Liberal party, Gunnar Helén, as well as both of his immediate predecessors (Sven Wedén and Bertil Ohlin), was similarly active in his party's youth organization during the initial stage of his political career.

STABILITY AND CHANGE

In every respect Sweden thus exemplifies a predominant participant political culture. Through mass membership in political parties and an impressive rate of electoral participation, the Swedes demonstrate a high degree of awareness about the system in general and an activist orientation toward the political process. The absence of political violence and the weakness of groups opposed in principle to the system also underscore an overwhelming popular commitment to participation within the established political framework.

Present forms of participation do not exclude qualitative changes in future modes of participation. Nor does the stability of political attitudes in Sweden imply rigidity of basic values and beliefs. On the contrary, the continuing cultural-political debate indicates a progressive transformation of attitudes and role expectations—as subsequent chapters will illustrate—that points beyond established patterns to new forms of participatory behavior.

THREE
TOWARD A PARTICIPATORY POLITICAL CULTURE
Elite values, social radicalism, and the new left

Political change rests on a reciprocal relation between elite and mass aspects of a nation's political culture. Within the framework of diffused political values and attitudes, the particular components of elite political culture provide the immediate criteria for determining the substance and form of a nation's politics. The pivotal role of political and organization leaders is most apparent in the modernization process. An elite that is principally committed to preserving its own social status and existing sociopolitical structures will be oriented toward system maintaining change. Conversely, a fragmented or unresponsive elite may unwittingly initiate regressive change with its accompanying manifestations of political chaos, attempted coups, and revolutions. Transformation is typically the product of concerted efforts by elites to achieve modernization, as in some of the nations of the third world, or their tacit endorsement of change instigated by innovating groups such as economic entrepreneurs.[1]

Popular attitudes are important as sources of positive or negative support for elite behavior. Systems in which a majority of citizens share the basic values of political and group leaders are

---

[1] On the relation between elites and innovating groups, see S. N. Eisenstadt, *Modernization: Protest and Change* (Englewood Cliffs, N.J.: Prentice-Hall, Inc., 1966), pp. 156–159.

obviously more cohesive than systems in which widespread opposition exists to established elites and political structures. The very existence of antisystem groups, on the other hand, may provide a stimulus for policy initiatives among national leaders that can culminate in new patterns of regressive, maintaining, or transforming change.

Elite political culture in Sweden constitutes a mix of positive and negative values that have proved conducive to system transformation throughout modern Swedish history.[2] The behavior of national leaders is characterized by "a highly pragmatic intellectual style, oriented toward the discovery of workable solutions to specific problems [that] structures a consensual approach to policy making."[3] Supporting elite consensus on transforming change are popular attitudes affirming industrialization, collective responsibility for individual security, and the redistribution of socioeconomic resources. Within the consensual norms of elite-mass values an inherent tension between opposing claims of collectivism and individualism provides a continuing impetus for political controversy and system change. This tension has assumed new manifestations during the past decade with the emergence of an activist minority of cultural and political radicals, whose attacks on fundamental tenets of the industrial-welfare state have helped promote the transition to postindustrial society.

SOCIOPOLITICAL DETERMINANTS OF ELITE ATTITUDES

During Sweden's economic and political modernization, the composition of the national elite underwent profound change. Whereas the rise of new sociopolitical forces has wrought revolution in many other countries, in Sweden the displacement of traditional leadership strata by leaders of modern political parties and an industrial economy ensued peacefully. Facilitating this process were persistent elite attitudes that remain characteristic attributes of contemporary Swedish political culture. These include moderation, pragmatism, and a willingness to seek compromise solutions to partisan differences.

[2] The concepts of positive and negative values are explored in detail in Gideon Sjoberg and Leonard D. Cain, "Negative Values, Countersystem Models, and the Analysis of Social Systems," in Herman Turk and Richard Simpson (eds.), *The Sociologies of Talcott Parsons and George C. Homans* (Indianapolis, Ind.: Bobbs-Merrill, 1971). Positive values, as the adjective implies, are affirmative in nature; negative values are those proscribing undesirable forms of behavior.

[3] Thomas J. Anton, "Policy," p. 99.

The emphasis on compromise as a principal hallmark of elite interaction in Sweden is, in the first instance, a product of the factors of national integration emphasized in preceding chapters. The attainment of political unity in the sixteenth century; well-established traditions of local and national government; and ethnic, linguistic, religious, and cultural homogeneity mitigated many potential sources of political conflict. Moreover, Sweden's small size and population have encouraged—as in Britain and the other Scandinavian countries—ease of communication and intimacy among members of the national leadership[4] As a restult a legacy of mutual tolerance, nurtured by close friendships and common class backgrounds, emerged that proscribed acrimonious debate and obstructionist behavior.

Economic and strategic imperatives have provided additional incentives for close cooperation among successive leadership generations. Because Sweden is so dependent on international trade for both the import of raw materials and the export of ore, timber, paper, and finished products, political and economic spokesmen confront a common necessity to harmonize partisan interests on behalf of maximum national benefits. Equally important, neutrality in foreign affairs underscored the necessity for conciliatory attitudes among political opponents, as a basis for national unity, in the face of recurrent European conflicts from the Austrian-Prussian occupation of Schleswig-Holstein in 1864 onward. Thus international economic and political considerations have dictated a pragmatic approach to national policies that complements underlying cultural predispositions toward compromise and cooperation.

The tradition of moderation among Swedish leaders has been encouraged by the fact that most leaders have had the kind of advanced education that stressed intellectual rather than demogogic skills. Most of the outstanding political figures of the nineteenth century, including Baron Louis De Geer (who was the architect of the parliamentary reform act of 1865–1866) and Hjalmar Branting (first chairman of the Social Democratic party), held university degrees. Even though social background characteristics of the national political leadership have changed significantly since the advent of parliamentarism and the extension of suffrage rights, education remains an important criterion of elite recruit-

---

[4] Dankwart A. Rustow, "Scandinavia: Working Multiparty Systems," in Sigmund Neumann (ed.), *Modern Political Parties* (Chicago: University of Chicago Press, 1956), p. 190.

ment. In the last nonsocialist cabinet to hold office prior to the Socialist rise to power in 1932, over 71 percent of the ministers had attended a university. This percentage fell to 58 during Hansson's first four years in office, and has remained relatively constant at that level throughout the Socialists' executive tenure. In 1970 university graduates numbered 11 among the 19 cabinet members.[5]

Positive elite attitudes embracing compromise and negative values restricting obstruction found policy expression in the successive reforms that accompanied political modernization. Responsive attitudes by traditional leaders to the demands of ascendant sociopolitical groups encouraged the latter to moderate their own behavior; thereby paving the way for institutionalized patterns of compromise in Sweden's modern political system.

EMULATION AND ASSIMILATION

Continuity of elite attitudes in Sweden was achieved through simultaneous processes of emulation and assimilation. In the first case the refusal of the nineteenth century bureaucratic-oligarchic elites to coerce their political opponents, which Robert Dahl suggests is one of the conditions for the emergence of a legitimate opposition,[6] provided a model of restraint that proponents of sociopolitical transformation internalized as their own norm of political behavior. In the second instance, the fact that the proponents of modernizing change only gradually displaced the traditional leadership spared Sweden a sudden transfer of authority that in other countries (notably in Weimar Germany) thwarted attempts at transforming change.

An important example of the transmission of elite attitudes through emulation was the evolution of socialist thought in Sweden. Ostensibly committed to the abolition of capitalism and the attainment of a classless society in accordance with orthodox Marxist tenets, early Swedish Socialist leaders nevertheless advocated a reformist policy from the beginning of the party's existence. Their program, strategy, and tactics reflected the absence of repressive government policies. In contrast, where repression did

---

[5] My calculations from *Sveriges Statskalender* and *Vem är det?*

[6] Robert A. Dahl, "Preface," in Dahl (ed.), *Political Oppositions in Western Democracies* (New Haven, Conn.: Yale University Press, 1966), p. xii.

exist—as in Czarist Russia and Imperial Germany—the socialist movements adopted a strikingly more militant stance against the established order.

The gradual rather than abrupt displacement of elite incumbents was the product of socioeconomic transformation. Throughout the nineteenth century Sweden's political leadership was composed largely of high-ranking civil servants. Lennart Linnarson has calculated that over 90 percent of the cabinet "united the country's highest civil and military administration and judicial authority with the realm's political leadership."[7] After the turn of the century, however, the composition of the national political elite began to change. Rather than resist emerging forces of industrialization and democratization, the bureaucratic elite willingly sought to assimilate representatives of the ascending sociopolitical forces within the leadership stratum. Thus for the first time spokesmen of the middle classes—including intellectuals, lawyers, and journalists who had "struggled in the first ranks for the new democratic and parliamentary ideas . . ."—came to be represented in the government.[8]

Emulative restraint on the part of the early reform leaders accelerated this process of assimilation. As Rustow notes in describing the initial appearance of Social Democrats in the Riksdag: "Conservative aristocrats might have been terrified at the thought of seeing the representatives of a professedly revolutionary labor movement intrude into the parliamentary inner sanctum. Yet their terror must have given way to agreeable surprise when the first intruder [Branting] turned out to be a highly educated, well-mannered gentleman who had gone to school together with the crown prince."[9]

As political leaders were increasingly drawn from the middle and lower classes, the high bureaucratic groups in the government steadily declined in importance. The visible break with Sweden's traditional oligarchical leadership occurred in 1917 with the formation of the Liberal-Social Democratic coalition. When a minority Social Democratic cabinet assumed office in 1920, the democratization of leadership recruitment was complete. Despite the recurrent rise and fall of successive Socialist, nonsocialist, and caretaker governments during the 1920s, political leadership had

---

[7] Lennart Linnarson, "Statsrådet i Sverige 1809–1934," in *De nordiska ländernas statsråd* (Uppsala: Statsvetenskapliga Föreningen, 1935), p. 24.

[8] Linnarson, p. 26.

[9] Rustow, *The Politics of Compromise* (Princeton, N.J.: Princeton University Press, 1955), p. 163.

irrevocably passed to the new pluralist forces of industrial-democratic Sweden.

Social Democratic preeminence since 1932 has led to a successive broadening of the base of political elite recruitment. (See Table 5.) Except for the years of wartime coalition, when Conservative, Liberal, and Center party membership in the cabinet increased the number of ministers with upper-class backgrounds, the general trend over the past four decades has been toward increased representation from the lower two social categories. Particularly striking is the rising curve of upward social mobility among cabinet members. More than half of the ministers who

Table 5   Classification of Ministers and Fathers by
Social Groups[a]

Period	Ministry	Number of Ministers	Social Status of Min.[b]				
			I	II	III	IV	Unknown
I 28-30	Lindman	13	5	8			
II 30-32	Ekman-Hamrin	14	4	8	2		
III 32-36	Hansson	13	2	10	1		
IV 36	Pehrsson i Bramstorp	12	3	9			
V 36-39	Hansson	14	3	10	1		
VI 39-45	Hansson	22	6	16			
VII 45-51	Hansson-Erlander	20	3	12	4	1	
VIII 51-57	Erlander	20	4	10	4	2	
IX 57-60	Erlander	24	3	13	5	2	1

[a]The data for 1928-1932 are derived from Linnarson, "Statsrådet i Sverige 1809-1934," in *De nordiska ländernas statsråd* (Uppsala: Statsvetenskapliga föreningen, 1935); subsequent figures are based on my own calculations from standard biographical references such as *Vem är det* [Who's Who] and *Vem var det* (Who Was Who).

[b]Explanation of social groups (adapted from Linnarson):

Group I: Highest public servants, leading individuals in either an independent position or the military, large estate owners as well as owners and leaders of the larger firms in business or industry; other persons without special qualifications who through birth or wealth belong to the leading ranks of society.

served in the Social Democratic cabinet after 1957 had lower-class social origins, compared to only 3 out of 12 members in the last nonsocialist government to hold office (that of the Center party in 1936).

Voluntarily relinquishing their political dominance in the wake of the electoral and parliamentary reforms from 1907 onward, members of the displaced conservative elite found recompense in a variety of positions of high social status. Some pursued eminent academic careers, while others attained leading positions in industry or in the civil service. Illustrative of the latter career pattern was Dag Hammarskjöld, whose father served as prime minister during World War I. A significant number of the traditional elite (or their descendants) became politically active in the modern era of parliamentarism. Two prime ministers during the

Period	Ministry	Number of Ministers	Social Status of Fathers				
			I	II	III	IV	Unknown
I 28–30	Lindman	13	4	6	3		
II 30–32	Ekman-Hamrin	14	4	6	2	2	
III 32–36	Hansson	13		3	6	3	1
IV 36	Pehrsson i Bramstorp	12	1	8	2	1	
V 36–39	Hansson	14	1	3	5	4	1
VI 39–45	Hansson	22	3	11	3	4	1
VII 45–51	Hansson-Erlander	20	2	3	5	9	1
VIII 51–57	Erlander	20	2	8	3	5	2
IX 57–60	Erlander	24	1	9	6	6	2

Group II: Other high public servants as well as principal assistant secretaries, district judges, mayors, professors, teachers with academic training, ministers and doctors; other officials; lawyers, journalists, engineers; other large businessmen, industrialists, and land-owners.

Group III: Public servants of lower rank; primary school teachers; lower officers in the military; smaller businessmen, artisans; farmers; trade unionists, and so forth.

Group IV: Soldiers, industrial workers, farm workers.

1920s—Baron Gerard Louis De Geer and Oscar von Sydow—claimed aristocratic origins, as does Palme, the present Social Democratic prime minister.

Hence, efforts by nineteenth-century conservatives to assimilate spokesmen of sociopolitical reform culminated in their own assimilation into Sweden's new democratic order. That the traditional elite was not violently deposed helped legitimize the peaceful transfer of authority to democratic-parliamentary leaders, thereby contributing to continuity in the historically and culturally defined elite attitudes of compromise and moderation.

SHARED POLITICAL VALUES

As persistent norms of political behavior, conciliatory attitudes among political antagonists have yielded a contemporary elite political culture that closely resembles the Anglo-American model of restraint, rational calculation, and a willingness to bargain with others in the pursuit of party or group goals.[10] These characteristics apply to formal political processes as well as interaction among pluralist forces within Sweden's broader socioeconomic system.

Although the postwar years have witnessed a succession of extended domestic conflicts, partisan spokesmen have repeatedly demonstrated their reluctance, as generations of leaders before them, "to draw the uttermost logical consequences from a principle."[11] Personal animosities and resentment surface in sometimes acerbic exchanges among group leaders, but Swedish leaders have persistently sought to resolve conflict within the framework of a general elite consensus affirming fundamental tenets of democratic government and decision processes.

One feature of political consensus in Sweden is a common commitment to parliamentarism. Once the principle of parliamentary government was introduced in 1917, all major parties joined in accepting it. Individual party members occasionally voiced dissatisfaction with the weakness of cabinet government during the 1920s,[12] but no organized force has avowedly rejected

---

[10] These characteristics of the "Anglo-American Political System" are elaborated by Gabriel Almond in "Comparative Political Systems," *The Journal of Politics*, 18 (August 1956), 398–400.

[11] Robert Michels, *Essays in Swedish History* (Minneapolis, Minn.: University of Minnesota Press, 1967), p. 11.

[12] Rustow, *The Politics of Compromise*, pp. 218–219.

parliamentarism in favor of an alternative form of government. So strongly has parliamentarism been established in Sweden that only in 1967–1969 was the constitution formally amended to incorporate explicit provisions for cabinet responsibility. Until then political precedent was the sole foundation on which parliamentary practice rested.

A second shared value is elite endorsement of pluralist structures and decision processes. Much of the electoral success of the Social Democrats, for example, can be attributed to their strategy of cooperation with private enterprise and the nonsocialist parties. Rather than nationalize major industries and credit institutions, Socialist leaders have pursued proclaimed party goals of sustained productivity and full employment through indirect fiscal and taxation policies, thereby leaving the principle of private ownership largely intact. Representatives of business interests have responded by providing a variety of positive supports for the government's economic measures, such as programs to retrain and relocate workers who are displaced from their earlier occupations by economic centralization, mergers, and automation. A reciprocal sense of trust similarly characterizes relations between the Swedish Federation of Trade Unions and the Swedish Employers' Association. Meeting at two- and three-year intervals to negotiate nation-wide wage agreements, the LO and the SAF view each other as respected and equal partners, with each according the other a legitimate role in promoting continued national economic growth.

Within parliament pluralism is institutionalized in the proportional distribution of committee seats and chairmanships among the Socialist and nonsocialist parties according to their respective electoral strength. Through regular leadership conferences, attended by the chairmen of the four major parties, government leaders attempt to keep the opposition informed of their policy intentions and to anticipate possible criticisms. Royal Commissions, which perform a key function in appraising policy alternatives during the circulatory stage of legislation, provide an additional avenue of pluralist participation in political decisions.

Underlying shared elite attitudes supportive of parliamentarism and pluralism are common beliefs in libertarianism and socioeconomic progress. With origins in ancient legal codes, judicial and constitutional guarantees of individual liberties are firmly sanctioned by centuries of tradition in Sweden. Fundamental civil liberties—freedom of speech, assembly, publication, and religious dissent—comprise an integral component of the modern Swedish political system, as witnessed by the virtual absence of political prosecution and official censorship. Belief in cumulative material and technological-scientific progress is exemplified by the willingness of political and organization leaders to promote continuing efforts to attain greater prosperity and a more rational allocation of physical and human resources.

Mass values and patterns of political behavior, discussed in the preceding chapter, provide strong supports for elite consensus in Sweden. Individual political competence and the high rate of electoral participation express popular affirmation of libertarianism and pluralist structures, while the persistent Socialist electoral plurality reflects widespread endorsement of comprehensive programs of economic, social, and political progress. The cohesiveness of elite-mass political attitudes has thus facilitated stable processes of system transformation in response to the requirements of continuing modernization. The perception of such requirements differs, however, according to conflicting assessments of collective versus individual priorities.

COLLECTIVISM AND INDIVIDUALISM

Throughout modern Swedish political history, conflict has been generated by contradictory claims advanced on behalf of collectivism and individualism. Both principles have served as the justification of transforming change, but often with significantly different policy implications. Although no group leaders have advocated one political orientation to the exclusion of the other, collectivist-individualist dualisms account in large measure for historical as well as contemporary ideological cleavages among Sweden's major sociopolitical forces.

Because neither concept has an unambiguous meaning, the ostensible tension between collectivist and individualist norms in Swedish politics is subject to differing interpretations. Kaj Björk, a prominent Social Democrat, has concisely delineated some of the difficulties in assessing their empirical manifestations in the evolution of Swedish ideological thought. During the economic and political transformation in the late nineteenth and early twentieth century, he observes,

[o]pposition movements lay behind the growth of various popular organizations such as the free-church movement, the temperance organizations, later the trade unions, cooperatives, and political

parties. These organizations were, however, collectivist associations that did not always display tolerance in their outward manifestations. Nevertheless, they sought by various means to achieve the liberation of the individual. A Conservative distrust of these popular movements was usually combined with reverence for the bureaucratic, oligarchical state and its ideology. Where, then, was individualism? Among the Conservatives or their organized opponents?[13]

Clearly, the answer is among both. Nevertheless differences in relative emphasis between collectivist and individual assumptions about the nature of society and politics produced discernible effects on the behavior of various party and group leaders. Drawing their ideological views from Marxist tenets that the individual's status and potential for self-realization are products of prevailing economic relations, the Social Democrats, the LO, and the Left Party-Communists have primarily espoused collectivist measures to promote their respective goals. In contrast spokesmen of the Liberal and Moderate Unity parties, as well as most economic interests, derive their socioeconomic and political doctrines from an individualistic theory of politics originating in the Enlightenment and classical liberalism.

This collectivist-individualist dualism constitutes the basic ideological division between "left" and "right" in modern Swedish politics. Emphasizing group solidarity as a means to mobilize support among industrial, agricultural, and white-collar workers, the Social Democrats and other forces on the left have persistently sought to attain positive conditions of individual security and relative socioeconomic equality. Accordingly they have advocated the primacy of collective responsibility in providing comprehensive welfare services, a more equitable distribution of income and taxation, and sustained economic growth. Among nonsocialist groups and parties, on the other hand, support for such collective measures is qualified by a continuing affirmation of individual initiative and the sanctity of private enterprise. Although first the Liberals and subsequently the Moderate Unity party have come to endorse Socialist-sponsored welfare programs and the necessity for government intervention in the economy, their contemporary leaders give ideological priority to the abolition of sociopolitical restraints on individual achievement rather than the extension of

---

[13] Kaj Björk, "Collectivism and Individualism," in M. Donald Hancock and Gideon Sjoberg (eds.), *Politics in the Post-Welfare State: Responses to the New Individualism* (New York: Columbia University Press, 1972), p. 249.

"solidarity politics." Between these polar views stands the Center party. Traditionally collectivist oriented in their defense of corporate agrarian interests, Center spokesmen have in recent years incorporated many of the individualist assumptions of "social liberalism," which are associated with the postwar Liberal party, into their own political program.

Mass attitudes toward welfare state policy reflect the collectivist individualist dualism among members of the political elite. According to survey data compiled during the 1960 election by Särlvik, 85 percent of a representative sample of voters who strongly endorsed the welfare state were Social Democrats. In contrast 50 percent of those who were opposed to it identified with the Moderate Unity party. Most Liberal and Center voters were either moderately or slightly opposed to the welfare state.[14]

Repeatedly these contradictory perspectives have clashed in successive domestic controversies and electoral campaigns. During their long tenure in executive office, the Social Democrats have acted on their advocacy of collectivist norms by initiating a series of economic, social, educational, and political reforms that have led to a steady expansion of the scope of government activity. While nonsocialist elites have actively supported many such initiatives, they have simultaneously attempted to modify Socialist policy in common opposition to what they perceive as an excessive emphasis on collectivism. Specifically they have based much of their agitation against the government party, in recent elections as well as in most of the major recent policy confrontations with the Social Democrats, on the alleged Socialist "concentration of power" at the apex of the political system.

Within the broader context of consensual attributes of Swedish political culture, the conflict between collectivist-individualist dualisms has resulted in a continuing reappraisal of the balance between centralized authority and decentralized responsibility. In the diffusion of various forms of political radicalism and the transformation of Sweden's multiparty system, as in national-local politics, are seen the empirical consequences of contemporary efforts to redefine that balance.

[14] Bo Särlvik, *The Role of Party Identification in Voters' Perception of Political Issues. A Study of Opinion Formation in Swedish Politics 1956–1961* (Göteborg: University of Göteborg, n.d.), p. 4. (Mimeographed.) Särlvik elaborates his findings in "Party Politics and Electoral Opinion Formation: A Study of Issues in Swedish Politics 1956–1960," *Scandinavian Political Studies*, 2 (New York: Columbia University Press, 1967).

THE MORAL-CULTURAL DEBATE

One of the unforeseen consequences of the maturation of the welfare state, which had been hailed by numerous social scientists and politicians as the triumph of administrative principles of rationality and efficiency over narrow claims of particular ideologies, was the emergence of a new radicalism in society and politics. Since the beginning of the 1960s diverse sociopolitical dissidents in Sweden, as elsewhere, have issued an open challenge to the established system. Splintered among competing factions and hardly espousing a united front of social criticism and innovation, the new radicals have nonetheless already exerted important effects on Sweden's political structures and processes. Their potential significance may prove even greater.

Rooted partly in international events such as mass opposition to American involvement in Vietnam, the Swedish variant of the new radical debate is by no means an isolated phenomenon. Having borrowed much of its terminology from movements and ideas that originated in other countries, such as American and continental European student agitation and neo-Marxist French thought, the new radicalism in Sweden seems even to lack originality. Yet the proponents of domestic reform have simultaneously drawn on indigenous traditions of sociopolitical debate in formulating and pressing their demands for change in existing values and policies. The result is a synthesis of views that is both at variance and consistent with Sweden's modern cultural and ideological heritage.[15]

Modern forms of social criticism in Sweden embrace complementary—and at times contradictory—features of apolitical and political reform efforts. Although both aspects of the new radicalism exhibit different dimensions, each has profoundly influenced the other. Cutting across the cultural and political boundaries of Sweden's new radicalism is a common moral concern with the relation of the individual to his social environment.

In Swedish literature and philosophy a dominant theme of critical reflections on morals and culture has consistently been alienation. As a focus of social criticism, alienation is, of course, by no means confined to Sweden. Conceived variously as the es-

[15] A penetrating critique of the Swedish New Left in light of indigenous traditions of radical debate is presented by Lars Gyllensten, "Swedish Radicalism in the 1960s: An Experiment in Political and Cultural Debate," in Hancock and Sjoberg.

trangement of the individual from the deity, society, and even himself, alienation is a concept virtually as ancient as recorded history itself. Throughout the evolution of Western civilization, artists and philosophers have persistently decried what they interpreted as man's progressive dehumanization and have propounded a variety of solutions intended to eliminate the various religious, social, and economic causes of that dehumanization. On a political level the increased mechanization of labor since the advent of the industrial revolution in eighteenth-century Britain has been traditionally viewed as one of the principal sources of alienation. Marx and Engels, in the *Communist Manifesto*, proclaim that workers have become an "appendage of the machine . . ." because labor has lost its individual character "and consequently all charm for the workman."

In more recent decades, many social critics have identified "mass society" as a primary cause of man's anomie. Ortega y Gasset sees in the rise of "hyperdemocracy," which he defines as the accession of the masses to complete social power, the threat of a "spiritual barbarism" devoid of a unifying moral code and hence destructive of higher social purposes.[16] In a similar vein, C. Wright Mills asserts that "the classical community of publics is being transformed into a society of masses, . . ."[17] with the sheer size of political and economic organizations destroying the individual's sense of "integrity" and reducing his role to monotonous routine.

Beginning in the 1880s with August Strindberg's exaltation of "a new and good society if only [man] could shake off the centuries-old accumulated weight of prejudice and tradition, . . ."[18] the indigenous Swedish cultural debate has reflected these concerns from abroad. As Gustafsson has observed:

> In long, sometimes slightly late and sometimes slightly watered down, but always openly accepted, waves, the ideas, styles, philosophies, artistic and literary movements of Europe have washed in over us. These have been actively received, transformed, and colored by our own conditions and, in a few cases, sent back in new forms.[19]

16 José Ortega y Gasset, *The Revolt of the Masses* (New York: W. W. Norton & Company, Inc., 1957), p. 11.

17 C. Wright Mills, *The Power Elite* (New York: Oxford University Press, 1956), p. 300.

18 Alrik Gustafson, *A History of Swedish Literature* (Minneapolis, Minn.: University of Minnesota Press, 1961), p. 245.

19 Lars Gustafsson, *The Public Dialogue in Sweden* (Stockholm: P. A. Norstedt & Söners Förlag, 1964), p. 7.

In the 1920s and 1930s, the cultural debate in Sweden centered on the conflict between social conservatism and radicalism. The latter was identified in a narrow sense with the proposals advanced by the Social Democrats for material improvements in social welfare and in broader perspective with the individual's liberation from conventional social and religious values.[20]

One of the most influential critics in prewar Sweden was Axel Hägerström (1868–1939), whose exposition of the relativity of value judgments[21] exerted a profound influence on the subsequent elaboration of secular ethics by such writers as Stig Dagerman (1923–1954) and Karl Vennberg (1910–   ). Both writers exemplified the mood of disillusionment that pervaded Swedish intellectual thought in the 1940s, in part wrought by the atrocities of World War II and Sweden's collective sense of guilt for escaping direct involvement. Vennberg's somber lyrics and Dagerman's writings, especially his pessimistic *Den dödsdömde* (*The Condemned*), were significant as expressions of social criticism because of their outspoken repudiation of what both authors viewed as oppressive (that is, conformist) mass norms.

In the post-World War II period, the research for new individual and social roles has assumed a variety of forms. A theme common to literary and philosophical writers, as well as visual artists, is experimentation. Examples include lyrical modernism, with its quest for new metaphors and structures, and the penetrating reexamination of individual motives in the films of Ingmar Bergman and Bo Widerberg.[22] Among leading novelists existentialism provides a major leitmotif, reflecting Swedish intellectual concern with moral issues posed by the wartime experience such as "freedom of choice and force, violence and non-violence, power and powerlessness and . . . the question of a meaningful life."[23]

One of the most responsive receptions to attempts to answer

[20] Gustafsson, pp. 9–10.

[21] Hägerström's seminal work was *Om moraliska föreställningars sanning* (On the Validity of Moral Conceptions), published in 1911.

[22] Contemporary lyrical modernists of special note are Per Olof Sundman. Birgitta Trotzig, Knut Nordström, Sven Fagerberg, Lars Gustafsson, and the German-Swedish writer, Peter Weiss. Bergman is best known for such films as *Smiles of a Summer Night, The Devil's Eye, The Seventh Seal, Wild Strawberries, The Virgin Spring, Through a Glass Darkly, Winter Light, The Silence, Persona, Hour of the Wolf,* and *Shame.* In contrast to Bergman's preoccupation with the difficulties of individual communication, Widerberg's emphasis—for example, in *Raven's End* and *The Ådalen Riots*—is on the status of industrial workers in modern society.

[23] Gustafsson, p. 10.

such questions was accorded Lars Gyllensten, a professor of medicine *cum* novelist, who in a series of essays and books has developed an existential doctrine of individual "liberation" and continual change as the only productive means to overcome estrangement in modern society. In his *Sokrates död* (*The Death of Socrates*), for example, Gyllensten elaborates the theme that men, like Socrates, unnecessarily become victims of their own convictions. "Nothing but evil comes from too firm convictions," Gyllensten has written. "If you only realize that the world doesn't want anything of you unless you fructify it with your own expectations and intentions, then you will be free."[24]

This shift in emphasis to experimentation and existential secular ethics reveals the extent to which the earlier controversy between conservatism and radicalism has been superceded by a debate on life in the kind of society the early radicals had sought to achieve. Thanks in no small part to the comprehensive reforms implemented under Social Democratic leadership during the previous three decades, most Swedes had attained by the early 1960s relative affluence and social security. Hence the paramount issue for Swedish intellectuals has become the appraisal of the *quality* of that life. For most writers and poets, this means a preoccupation with the self, including efforts to maximize individual aesthetic consciousness and reflective insights. But for others—especially those inclined toward political activism—the necessary objective of qualitative change is group action on behalf of other levels of the individual's potential for self-fulfillment, namely the attainment of greater economic and social freedom.

SOCIAL RADICALISM

The effects of Sweden's moral-cultural debate on general public attitudes are at best diluted and fragmentary. The active participants in the debate are few in number, and their views are not representative of what Gyllensten describes as a "more conservative and eclectic point of view . . ." among the population at large.[25] If only indirectly, however, the ideas of the creative intelligentsia have influenced general trends of continuing social

[24] Quoted in Gustafsson, pp. 36–37.
[25] Gyllensten, p. 280.

change in Sweden. For a great many Swedes, concepts of a secular ethic, derived in part from the intellectual debate and emphasizing the primacy of individual moral choice, have been translated into new and, in comparison with traditional mores, radical standards of social behavior.

Sweden's new social radicalism exhibits numerous facets. In the religious sphere radical ferment extends from continued demands for a complete separation of church and state to youthful agitation to politicize the dissenting free church movement as a forum of attack "against established society and capitalism in the third world."[26] With respect to required religious training in schools, adult and student critics alike advocate that the present instruction in orthodox Christian doctrines be abandoned altogether or transformed into surveys of the world religions and philosophies.

Censorship and invasion of individual privacy, for example, through the use of cameras and electronic listening devices, are additional objects of radical debate. While the state imposes virtually no restrictions on the right of publication, including pornography, movies remain subject to review by a government board. When scenes from the film *491* were ordered cut in 1964, dissident publicists charged the board with exercising a double standard. They pointed out that movies directed by Bergman, who enjoys an international reputation, were never censored while those by lesser-known figures, in this case Vilgot Sjöman, were.[27] In their view, all censorship should be abandoned in favor of the individual's right to view what he wishes. Similarly, the sanctity of individual freedom has been upheld in the face of restrictive government surveillance measures. A case in point was opposition among members of the informed public to the policy of the Swedish police of photographing persons frequenting reputed homosexual centers in Stockholm and other large cities. Such practices, they argued, posed a potential threat of incrimination to innocent individuals. The result, in this instance, was government compliance.

The most touted illustration of social radicalism in Sweden, from the perspective of outside observers, is the sexual revolution. Often sensationalized in the foreign press, the liberalization of sexual mores in Sweden—and in Scandinavia as a whole—consti-

---

[26] *Dagens Nyheter*, March 17, 1969.
[27] Subsequently Sjöman has acquired an international reputation in his own right with the production of *I Am Curious (Yellow)* and *I Am Curious (Blue)*.

tutes a search for honesty in interpersonal relations rather than the onslaught of wholesale promiscuity.[28] A secular ethic of individual choice and responsibility for one's own actions has increasingly displaced traditional religious and social dicta as criteria of behavior, resulting in a progressive transformation of sexual attitudes and the tenor of the public sexual debate.

Survey research has documented changes in both individual sexual practices and the nature of the ethical standards that govern them. A study in 1964, conducted among 18-year-old secondary school students in Örebro, revealed "that 57 percent of the boys had experienced intercourse, the median age for first coitus being 16. The figure of the girls was 46 percent and the median age 17. In the vast majority of the cases first intercourse was between boys and girls who were 'going steady' or knew each other very well."[29] In 1966–1969, Dr. Hans Zetterberg, Director of the Swedish Institute for Public Opinion Research (SIFO), conducted a comprehensive survey of sexual habits among a national sample of 1952 Swedes. According to his findings, 57 percent of the men and 44 percent of the women had had sexual intercourse before the age of 18, and 85 percent and 82 percent, respectively, had experienced intercourse before they reached 20.[30] In terms of ethical valuations concerning sexual behavior, Zetterberg found that 93 percent of all Swedes accept sexual relations between persons who are engaged or "going steady," but, significantly, that an equal percentage disapprove of promiscuity both before and after marriage.[31]

This "revolution" in sexual behavior has helped prompt a searching debate on sex education in the schools, Swedish laws concerning abortion, and sexual roles in society. Compulsory sex education was first introduced in school curricula in the 1940s, and became a required subject in 1956. Originally designed to provide factual information about conception and childbirth as well as instruction in prevailing (or "official") morality, such as proscriptions against premarital sex, sex education courses have come under attack from a variety of quarters. Some, including a group of Swedish doctors, have advocated greater emphasis on the

[28] Björk and Gyllensten in Hancock and Sjoberg.

[29] Birgitta Linnér, *Society and Sex in Sweden* (Stockholm: The Swedish Institute, 1967), p. 16.

[30] J. Robert Moskin, "The New Contraceptive Society," *Look* (February 1969), p. 80.

[31] Moskin, p. 53.

moral implications of sexual practices. Others, including spokesmen for the Swedish Union of Secondary School Students, demand
that ethical considerations be relegated entirely to individual con-
sciences. Moreover, student leaders have urged that greater attention be given in class to the use of contraceptives. In general the
response of national education authorities in Sweden to the continuing controversy over compulsory sex education has been to
adopt—with some reservations—a more liberal approach toward
questions of ethical evaluation.

Radical dissent concerning legal codes on abortion centers on
efforts to remove remaining restrictions on the right of abortion.
Therapeutic abortion was legalized in 1938, but a committee of
doctors appointed by the National Board of Health must grant
approval, based primarily on considerations of a woman's physical and mental health, before an operation can be performed. The
resulting delays, and the possibility that an application may be
denied, force at least hundreds (if not thousands) of women annually to undergo illegal abortions, often under no qualified medi-
cal supervision. To eliminate such harmful practices, various
groups have championed for decades the absolute right of a
woman to a legal abortion. In light of government reluctance to
liberalize present laws, young Liberals in the 1960s began organiz-
ing chartered flights for pregnant women to Poland, where legal
provisions on abortion are less stringent than in Sweden.

The sexual revolution has also cast the struggle for women's
rights into new perspective. Despite significant gains in the legal
and economic status of women during the present century, they
have not in practice attained complete equality with men. Women
are still excluded from important jobs, such as offices in the higher
civil service; they are underrepresented in most positions of leadership; and they do not always receive equal pay for equal work.
To the extent that the new secular ethic in sexual mores embraces
respect for women as persons rather than objects, radical efforts
led by the Liberal and Social Democratic youth associations to
equalize professional opportunities and remuneration for women
have gained increased momentum.

Finally, social radicalism is manifest in additional types of
behavior that most Swedes view as overtly antisocial. A leading
example is the increased use of drugs, especially marijuana and
amphetamines, among the nation's youth. An estimated 10,000 to
12,000 persons had become amphetamine addicts by 1970,
prompting an intensive debate on means of treatment and drug

control.[32] One Swedish expert on drug abuse has suggested that the government "may find it necessary to establish 'drug islands,' where addicts could volunteer to spend their lives, while being cared for by the state and given all the drugs they want."[33]

CHALLENGE TO COMPLACENCY: THE NEW LEFT

The social dimensions of Sweden's new radicalism have animated public discussion across established group and political boundaries. Proponents of reform as well as defenders of the *status quo* are found in all of the major political parties, professional and voluntary associations, and various religious bodies. While differences of opinion concerning religious, censorship, and sexual issues are real, particularly between generations, most Swedes are willing to concede that the terms of such debate are consonant with liberal-socialist traditions of radical reform that infused Swedish thought from the mid-nineteenth century onward. In Sweden's contemporary welfare state, agitation to achieve further liberation from social or legal restraints on individual preferences, life styles, and career opportunities therefore involves *degrees* of modification in established behavior patterns and laws rather than the substitution of one set of principles for another.

The same generalization does not entirely hold for the political expressions of radical controversy. Sharing much of the same moral fervor that permeates the cultural-social debate, advocates of *political* change have concentrated more on redefining group relations in society than on the individual per se. Divided among radical liberals and neo-Marxists, Sweden's political radicals seek in common the basic transformation of existing pluralist structures and processes.

Paradoxically, postwar political stability—a product of affluence and the success of comprehensive welfare measures—has provided an important stimulus for the rise of political radicalism. Among some members of the intellectual-political "establishment," the decline of traditional forms of ideological debate in Sweden was initially interpreted as the genesis of a new era of mass consensus on pluralist-welfare society. The most articulate proponent of this view was Herbert Tingsten. One of Sweden's leading social critics and former editor of the second largest Lib-

---

[32] *The New York Times*, April 10, 1970, p. 41.
[33] *The New York Times*, April 10, 1970, p. 41.

eral daily newspaper, *Dagens Nyheter*, Tingsten has characterized the trend toward compromise among the established political parties as "the death of ideology, a fusion of general ideas. The old [emotionally] charged words, conservatism, liberalism, socialism, are still used, . . . but they are no longer applicable as systems of preconceived notions of what will happen and what should be done."[34] Parallel with this process, Tingsten states, "viewpoints and values have become so reduced in importance that one . . . can speak of a development from politics to administration, from principles to techniques."[35]

Numerous other writers, including S. M. Lipset, Daniel Bell, and Manfred Friedrich, have elaborated comparable themes elsewhere. Their pronouncements on the "end-of-ideology" reflect parallel developments during the 1950s and early 1960s in a number of modern welfare societies. Throughout Scandinavia, as in Germany, Great Britain, and the United States, economic growth coupled with the extension of welfare services had engendered an unprecedented era of broad political agreement on ultimate policy goals.

Implicitly agreeing with much of Tingsten's analysis, spokesmen for emerging forces of political dissent in Sweden nevertheless have drawn opposite conclusions. On one level, the pervasiveness of compromise as a principal hallmark of Swedish politics has prompted an emotional reaction to established political patterns. Experiencing either the frustration of boredom or moral indignation because of their belief that humanistic values have been sacrificed at the altar of political expediency, many Swedes have become increasingly disaffected with the tranquillity of a well-managed and prosperous society. While intellectual malaise in politics is by no means a new phenomenon, incipient dissatisfaction with the apparent success of the Swedish welfare state has provided an important catalyst for the subsequent elaboration of critical insights into some of its underlying weaknesses. For, on a more penetrating level of analysis, the welfare state contains a number of serious shortcomings. The most significant of these is the growing contradiction between the proclaimed ideals of pluralist-welfare society and actual system performance.

---

[34] Tingsten, *Från idéer till idyll* (Stockholm: P. A. Norstedt & Söners Förlag, 1966), p. 18. An earlier exposition of Tingsten's views is found in his *Demokratiens problem*, rev. ed. (Stockholm: Bokförlaget Aldus/Bonniers, 1960). He defends his thesis against domestic criticism in *Strid kring idyllen* (Stockholm: P. A. Norstedt & Söners Förlag, 1966).

[35] Tingsten, *Från idéer till idyll*, p. 18.

Despite affluence, over a third (37.9 percent) of the total working force earns less than $2000 a year. Among these nearly 300,000 Swedes have an annual income below $600—well under minimum subsistence requirements.[36] While welfare services help alleviate abject poverty, the fact remains that many Swedes—particularly the poorly educated, the elderly, and the handicapped—do not share the socioeconomic security that prosperity affords the majority of citizens. Exacerbating the problem of depressed wages is continued job insecurity for many semiskilled or unskilled laborers in areas where private businesses have been forced to close down or consolidate.

Within this political sphere as well as in professional associations, the democratic ideal of individual efficacy in the decision process has been diluted by a continuing trend toward the bureaucratization of politics. One illustration, in terms of the formal political system, is the postwar rationalization of local government structures.[37] Whereas political authorities have been able to justify the merger of primary municipalities into larger units in the name of administrative efficiency, the consequence for many Swedes is to lessen their sense of identity with local government. Nationally, the elaboration of welfare services has provided additional restrictions on the ability of individuals to exert a meaningful influence on political processes. In that the efficient administration of complex welfare programs requires the skills of a growing number of experienced but anonymous civil servants, Sweden's political apparatus has assumed an increasingly remote bureaucratic character.

Nor have the political parties escaped comparable tendencies toward bureaucratization. Confirming Robert Michels' "iron law of oligarchy," party structures have become largely centralized and subject to the dominance of their respective leaders in parliament. One indication of the entrenched authority of established party leadership echelons is a gradual increase in the average age of members within the various parliamentary factions. Between 1937 and 1961, the average age of Riksdag deputies rose from 50.1 years to 52.4. In 1961 only 6 percent of the representatives were 39 years old or younger, with the highest number (42.2 percent) between the ages of 50 and 59.[38]

---

[36] *Statistisk årsbok 1968*, p. 346.

[37] See Chapter Four.

[38] Lars Sköld and Arne Halvarson, "Riksdagens sociala sammansättning under hundra år," in Arthur Thomson (ed.), *Samhälle och riksdag*, I (Stockholm: Almqvist & Wiksell, 1966), pp. 447 and 449.

Simultaneously, private associations have undergone comparable processes of structural rationalization and centralization of decision-making authority. Local unions have lost virtually all autonomy within the LO, while the Consumer Cooperative Association, which included 338 member societies in 1965, has initiated a process of internal consolidation that envisages the creation of 15 to 25 national societies by the mid-1970s.[39]

In light of remaining disparities in wages and freedom from socioeconomic insecurity, political dissidents in Sweden could thus cogently argue that the welfare state had failed to achieve its ostensible objectives of equality and social justice. Moreover, the accelerating bureaucratization of politics, in both the public and private spheres, seemed to negate even basic premises of political democracy such as the capacity of voters or members of groups to make relevant choices among policy alternatives. From the critical perspective of those who questioned the assumption of Tingsten and others that the welfare state had succeeded in solving most socioeconomic and political issues, therefore, ideology was demonstrably not yet "dead." On the contrary, the persisting contradictions in welfare society seemed to necessitate the resurgence of ideological consciousness as a basis for future political action to resolve such contradictions.[40]

In response to the perception of major shortcomings in Swedish society, diverse groups of political radicals initiated in the early 1960s multiple demands for basic sociopolitical change. Among nonsocialist activists, led principally by members of the Liberal and Center party youth associations, the major focus of radical dissent was opposition to centralizing tendencies within the political system. In the daily press, books, and within the nonsocialist parties themselves, young Liberals and Centrists such as Per Ahlmark and Göran Josefsson advocated a concerted effort by both parties to promote "progressive social liberalism." Their specific proposals for domestic reforms included the need to broaden the influence of party and organization members on group decisions, rejuvenate party leadership, and attain greater equality in social relations.[41]

[39] Nils Elvander, "Democracy and Large Organizations," in Hancock and Sjoberg, pp. 303–304.

[40] This is the thesis argument in Kurt Samuelsson, *Är ideologierna döda* (Stockholm: Bokförlaget Aldus/Bonniers, 1966).

[41] Such demands for domestic reform are advanced in two collections of essays by members of the Liberal and Center parties: Per Ahlmark, *et al.*, *Mitt i 60-talet* (Stockholm. Bonniers, 1965) and Per Ahlmark (ed.), *Många liberaler* (Stockholm: Bonniers, 1966).

The most militant attack on the system came from the neo-Marxist New Left. To a far greater extent than was true of the radical liberals, dissidents within the Communist and Social Democratic parties seized on the contradictions of Sweden's pluralist-welfare society to articulate a comprehensive ideological critique of the established order. Influenced by international events such as Khrushchev's anti-Stalinist campaign, the growth of polycentrism in Eastern Europe, and the diffusion of revisionist thought among the Communist parties in Western Europe, the Swedish New Left emerged as an ideological movement that sought to combine loyalty to the fundamental principles of classical Marxism with a repudiation of the rigid bureaucratic rule associated with institutionalized communism. In this regard the New Left assimilated essentially the same ideological characteristics as both the Socialist People's parties that had been founded in the early 1960s in Denmark and Norway and radical student leaders in France and Germany. Like such groups in other European countries, New Left spokesmen in Sweden were also able to capitalize on a rising wave of mass demonstrations against American policies in Vietnam to press their claims for domestic transformation.

In contrast to New Left movements on much of the continent and in the United States, however, the Swedish New Left confronted the paradoxical situation that a Social Democratic party had exercised executive authority for over three decades. Ostensibly, therefore, the political condition for a radical transformation of domestic society on behalf of mass democratic (as opposed to "minority capitalist") interests had already been met. To the extent that the Social Democrats based much of their success in office on pragmatic rather than ideologically "pure" policies, however, the New Left maintained that the governing party had in fact betrayed the real interests of Sweden's working classes. Hence, New Left spokesmen resolved the apparent paradox that socialism had not been achieved in Sweden despite long-term Social Democratic rule with the theory of "bourgeois hegemony," a concept derived from French neo-Marxist thought. Because "monopoly capitalists" controlled the economy, the New Left argued, the bourgeoisie still dominated society and indirectly the political system as well.[42]

Thus from the New Left point of view, the greatest weakness of Sweden's pluralist-welfare society was the failure of the Social Democrats to extend democratic principles from the political

[42] Gyllensten, pp. 287–283.

sphere to economic and social relations. Herein the New Left perceived the cause of all contradictions in the domestic system, from inequality in wages and women's rights to the alienation of individuals from bureaucratizing tendencies in politics and private organizations. Eliminating such contradictions required not partial reforms in the tradition of the majority Social Democrats and radical liberalism, but a comprehensive restructuring of the entire society in accordance with the tenets of classical Marxism.

Until the advent of the New Left the only radical left alternative to the policies of the Social Democrats was the miniscule Communist party. Yet the Swedish Communists had long ceased to provide a significant impetus for sociopolitical change. Instead, the party had become an ineffectual outlet for protest votes, aggregating an average electoral following of only 5.2 percent since the end of World War II. Pursuing a domestic policy of conciliation toward the Social Democrats, Communist leaders had concentrated much of their agitprop efforts on foreign policy issues, in particular the defense of Soviet foreign policies in Eastern Europe.

As the major repository of revolutionary rhetoric and Socialist consciousness, the Communist party nevertheless constituted a logical vehicle for the New Left attack against Sweden's "bourgeois hegemony." To transform the party into an effective instrument of sociopolitical change, New Left opposition forces began in the early 1960s an open debate within party ranks on what they believed to be the causes of Communist atrophy in Sweden.[43]

Through the columns of the Communist newspaper, *Ny Dag*, they focused their criticism on the party's role as unswerving apologist for policies pursued by the Soviet Union and the "people's democracies." The critics charged that the party had isolated itself from the Swedish workers because of its earlier defense of Stalin and its more recent endorsement of the suppression of the Hungarian revolution by the Soviet Union and the erection of the Berlin Wall by the East German regime. In claiming that the overwhelming majority of the Swedish electorate therefore viewed the party as "unreliable," the New Left critics were expressing bitter dissatisfaction with the established party leadership. Urging that the party rejuvenate its image and appeal, New Left spokes-

[43] Åke Sparring (ed.), *Kommunism en i Norden* (Stockholm: Bokförlaget Aldus/Bonniers, 1965), p. 31. A more extended analysis of the transition of Communist ideology in Sweden is Sparring, *Från Höglund till Hermansson. Om revisionismen i Sveriges kommunistiska parti* (Stockholm: Albert Bonniers Förlag, 1967).

men began to agitate for free criticism of the socialist systems in the Soviet Union, Eastern Europe, and China, and called for Communist endorsement of civil liberties and a multiparty system in Sweden.[44]

Ideological renewal emerged as the dominant theme of the party's twentieth congress in January 1964, when C. H. Hermansson, editor-in-chief of *Ny Dag*, was elected the new party chairman. Forty-seven years old, an astute theoretician, and one of parliament's most talented debaters, Hermansson proved an ideal choice in the eyes of the younger dissidents. In a keynote address to the convention, Hermansson emphasized the necessity of regeneration in Communist policies to mobilize expanded membership and new sources of electoral support. Sharply criticizing the Social Democrats for their "complacency, even negative attitude toward nationalization," Hermansson called for increased "democratic controls" over the economy through selective nationalization and the expansion of producers' cooperatives.[45] "Until now the Social Democrats have governed *with* big business," he declared. "We believe it is time for the Swedish government to implement policies aimed *against* big business and its power."[46]

While Hermansson's views of ultimate Communist goals to "democratize" industry did not differ significantly from the party's traditional ideological principles, his stress on innovation in methods to achieve them reflected the New Left insistence on an experimental and nondogmatic transition to socialism. He pointed out that the Swedish Communists

> cannot ignore the rich experience that has been provided by the successful struggle the working-class had led to achieve Socialism in other countries. But the forms and methods successfully employed . . . in another historical milieu . . . cannot be decisive in our own. . . . The proletarian revolution and triumph of Socialism will display a wide range of variations [in different countries]. We will make our contribution to the victory of the international working-class by finding the best means of success . . . to build Socialism in our own country.[47]

[44] Letter by Harald Rubinstein in *Ny Dag* on September 30, 1963. Quoted in Sparring, *Kommunismen i Norden*, pp. 38–40.

[45] Sveriges kommunistiska parti, 20:a kongressen, *För vidgat folkstyre—mot storfinansen* (Stockholm: Sveriges kommunistiska parti, 1964), p. 39.

[46] *För vidgat folkstyre—mot storfinansen*, p, 44. Italics in the original.

[47] *För vidgat folkstyre—mot storfinansen*, p. 71. For an elaboration of Hermansson's views, see C. H. Hermansson, *Vänsterns väg* (Stockholm: Rabén & Sjögren, 1965).

The victory of the "democratic opposition" over the discredited party leadership signaled the formal emergence of the New Left as an institutionalized political force in Sweden. Symbolically this fact was underscored three years later when the executive committee voted to change the official name of the party to Left Party-Communists.

TOWARD A PARTICIPATORY POLITICAL CULTURE

The simultaneous manifestations of radical political dissent among nonsocialist and neo-Marxist critics revealed new limits of consensus in Swedish politics. On both the right and left, the achievements of a gradualist policy of reform, largely initiated by the Social Democrats but endorsed in principle by leaders of the parliamentary opposition, were not received with uncritical acceptance. On the contrary, the very success of the Swedish welfare system, which had exposed in increasingly sharp focus contradictions between democratic ideals of equality and the reality of inequality, appeared to open new possibilities for more comprehensive future change.

Like the participants in the cultural-moral debate, Sweden's new political radicals constituted only a small minority of the general population. But in contrast to the diffused influence of the intellectual minority the long-term consequences of political agitation could potentially affect the mass of citizens in a direct and unequivocal manner. Whereas members of the intelligentsia speculated on means to enhance individual moral consciousness and existential freedom, the self-appointed leaders of political radicalism sought basic changes in patterns of political and economic group interaction.

Despite their fundamental difference of emphasis, the major themes of cultural-social and political radicalism during the 1960s in Sweden served complementary functions in helping redefine the nature of collective-individual relations in modern welfare society. On one hand, collective guarantees of relative affluence and security had increased the scope of individual experimentation and self-realization. Yet, on the other, the bureaucratization of politics and the absence of direct social controls over industry had led to a reappraisal of the collectivity itself. Radical liberals sought to make the political collectivity more flexible by expanding the scope of participation in group (especially party) decisions, while neo-Marxists established the "democratization" of the economy on a decentralized model of Socialism as the more urgent task.

Emerging from these contributions to renewed social and ideological controversy was a discernible shift from satisfaction with formal rights of individual freedom. Despite the conflicting priorities of sociopolitical reform among diverse proponents of change, radical dissent pointed beyond representative democracy and the established pluralist system toward a participatory (as distinct from participant) political culture in which individuals would attain more immediate influence on the social, political, and economic terms of their day-to-day existence.

FOUR
THE COMMUNAL LINK
Local government and national politics

As Sweden is a unitary state, with constitutional authority concentrated in the hands of the national parliament and executive, provincial and municipal administrative units lack the independence of state governments in federal systems such as the United States or West Germany. Nevertheless local governments perform major functions in modern Swedish politics, implementing the bulk of day-to-day domestic policies.

As a principal instrument of policy administration, local government provides a salient example of the dialectical interplay between prevailing patterns of elite consensus and cleavage in Sweden. Consensual norms are evidenced in the importance that political leaders jointly accord regional-municipal structures as well as in the style of local politics. Partisan differences have emerged with respect to the evolution of national-local relations, as witnessed by party disputes over particular policies and a prolonged constitutional controversy over restructuring the "communal link" with the national political system.

THE STRUCTURAL FRAMEWORK

Formal political responsibility for supervising and coordinating domestic policies in Sweden is centralized among the 12 departments that make up the Royal Chancery in Stockholm.[1] Actual

---

[1] See Chapter Seven.

policy implementation, however, is assigned an interlocking web of independent administrative agencies[2] and regional-municipal political units. The latter constitute Sweden's system of local government.

The functional decentralization of administrative services among local authorities has evolved from a tradition of community gatherings to discuss matters of common concern that dates from the pagan era in Swedish history. From the twelfth century onward, church parishes assumed responsibility for local affairs—including education and poor relief—in addition to their ecclesiastical duties. Reforms of 1817 and 1842 established local secular political assemblies and a national school system, and in 1862 the national government created by royal decree new provincial governments (*län*) alongside the existing rural and city districts. A number of revisions have been made in intervening years that have redefined the activities and boundaries of local government, but the present system retains the basic features of the 1862 reform.

Local government in contemporary Sweden therefore consists of a two-tiered structure with 25 provincial governments serving as the principal intermediary link between national political authorities and the rural-urban municipalities.[3] Until recently Stockholm and five other cities (Göteborg, Malmö, Hälsingborg, Norrköping, and Gävle) were accorded special autonomy as urban provincial districts because of their population densities. During the 1960s, Stockholm, Hälsingborg, Norrköping, and Gävle merged with surrounding provinces, leaving only Göteborg and Malmö with separate administrative status. Other local units with specialized functions include 81 tax commissioner districts, 119 police districts, and 122 national registration districts.

Provincial government functions primarily to administer hospital and mental health facilities, dental clinics, children's homes, the folk high schools, and vocational training. These services are carried out by provincial agencies, local offices of the national administrative boards, and the local municipalities. Most policy directives are issued by the central government, but the provinces exercise discretionary authority in some aspects of education and social welfare.

---

[2] See Chapter Eight.

[3] The provincial governments include Stockholm, Uppsala, Södermanland, Östergötland, Jönköping, Kronoberg, north Kalmar, south Kalmar, Gotland, Blekinge, Kristianstad, Malmöhus, Halland, Göteborg and Bohus, Älvsborg, Skaraborg, Värmland, Örebro, Västmanland, Kopparberg, Gävleborg, Västernorrland, Jämtland, Västerbotten, and Norrbotten.

The ranking executive official in each of the 25 provinces is the provincial governor (*landshövdning*), who is appointed by the national executive for life tenure. As the central government's highest administrative representative in the various provinces, the governor supervises policy implementation through appointed provincial administrative officials (*länsstyrelsen*). Legislative authority is vested in the provincial assembly (*landsting*), whose members are elected for three-year terms on the basis of proportional representation. The deputies choose a provincial executive committee (*förvaltningsutskott*) that coordinates regional policies in cooperation with the governor and administrative personnel.

In addition to their deliberative function, the provincial assemblies served until 1971 as electoral colleges for the election of representatives to the upper chamber of the Riksdag. For this purpose the provincial assemblies and the larger urban provincial assemblies formed nineteen constituencies that were grouped into eight districts with approximately equal population. At eight-year intervals each district elected, on a rotation basis, one eighth of the 151 members of the first chamber. Thus one eighth of the upper chamber's membership was renewed annually.

Local government units are classified according to population density as rural communes (*landskommun*), mixed rural-urban boroughs (*köping*), and cities (*stad*). Originally corresponding to traditional church parish boundaries, over 3000 primary municipalities existed as late as the 1940s. Through parliamentary legislation and voluntary mergers, the number declined to 905 by 1968. This total includes 675 rural communes, 93 boroughs, 132 cities, and 5 municipalities with limited communal rights. The projected goal of structural rationalization is 282 communal blocs by the end of the 1970s.

The municipalities are primarily concerned with the administration of national legislation governing public health, elementary and secondary education, housing, highway construction, and social welfare. Popularly elected assemblies (which are called *kommunalfullmäktige* in the communes and boroughs and *stadsfullmäktige* in the cities) also enact policy dealing with purely local matters such as land purchase for industry and municipal housing, public utilities, fire protection, and cultural, social, and athletic facilities.

Like delegates to the provincial assemblies, members of the municipal assemblies are elected for three-year terms according to proportional representation. The number of representatives varies from 15 to 60, depending on the population in a given commune or city. The assemblies select an executive committee (*kom-*

munalnämnden or *drätselkammeren*), generally composed of five to eleven members, that steers the work of the assembly and oversees policy administration. In contrast to most cities in the United States, there is no equivalent to the office of mayor in the urban districts. The national cabinet appoints a chief magistrate (*borgmästare*) in each city among candidates who are nominated by the local assembly, but his role is that of judge rather than executive officer.

Government services on both the provincial and municipal levels are financed by taxes on individual and corporate earnings, direct subsidies by the central government, and revenue from public housing and utilities. In 1966 local government income totaled 22,866 million crowns (approximately $4573 million). Taxes provided the largest source: 69 percent in the case of the provincial governments and 49 percent in the primary municipalities and cities. Government subsidies constituted 15 percent and 19 percent, respectively; the remainder was derived primarily from public owned services.[4]

COORDINATION OF LOCAL POLITICS

Particularism is not a salient feature of local politics in Sweden. In some regions, especially Skåne in the south and Gotland in the Baltic, distinctive speech patterns and semiautonomous historical traditions perpetuate a discernible regional identity. But provincialism exists only in a diluted form, and does not impede the close coordination of national and local policy.

One factor mitigating political separatism is Sweden's communications structure. Radio and television are state monopolies, organized as private companies but broadcasting the same program simultaneously throughout the entire country. With few exceptions, the major newspapers—including *Dagens Nyheter, Expressen, Svenska Dagbladet*, and *Aftonbladet*—are centered in Stockholm and claim a national circulation.[5] Nearly all are identified with one of the five principal parties. Out of 152 newspapers published in 1967 only 21 were classified as independent.[6]

Even more significant is the combination of legal and politi-

---

[4] Totals and percentages are calculated from *Statistisk årsbok 1968*, pp. 398–406.

[5] The major exceptions are the progressive conservative *Sydsvenska Dagbladet* and *Kvällsposten* in Malmö and the liberal *Göteborgs-Posten* in Göteborg. The large Stockholm dailies have regional printing offices and usually print special sections devoted to local news.

[6] *Statistisk årsbok 1968*, p. 340.

cal factors that insures the integration of local government into the national political system. In the first instance, the provinces and municipalities are constitutionally subordinate to the authority of the central government. Hence the Riksdag and the national executive, rather than the local assemblies themselves, exercise ultimate control over policy guidelines and local government structures. Their legal subordination is further underscored by the fact that the cabinet appoints the provincial governors and chief magistrates.

Politically, postwar legislation establishing uniform state-sponsored services throughout the country has progressively transformed local government into an administrative extension of the central government. Leading examples include provisions for communal support for home construction (1947); expanded welfare and public health programs (1956, 1958, and 1960); and educational reform (1950 and 1962). As a result the traditional distinction between strictly local policies and statutory functions imposed by the Riksdag "has . . . lost much of its practical importance."[7]

Also contributing to the coordination of national and local policies is the Swedish party system. Although a few local parties exist in individual communes or municipalities, their aggregate following comprises less than 1 percent of the electorate. The Swedish party system is wholly national in scope, with all of the five established parties maintaining organizations in each district to recruit members and mobilize popular support. Their centralized bureaucracies and a constant flow of communication between the local organizations and national headquarters in Stockholm provide a significant integrative link between the provincial-local echelons of government and the national political system.[8]

SERVICE AND POLITICAL FUNCTIONS OF LOCAL GOVERNMENT

Given this framework of legal-political coodination, the degree of local political autonomy is clearly restricted. Nevertheless the service and political functions of local government are significant in their own right. Since the advent of modernization the scope of

[7] Sweden, Justitiedepartementet, *Statens offentliga utredningar 1965:54, Författningsfrågan och det kommunala sambandet* (Stockholm: Justitiedepartementet, 1965), p. 39. Hereafter referred to as *SOU 1965:54*.

[8] That local party structures are not wholly dominated by the national organizations, however, is indicated by the independent move of Conservative leaders toward nonsocialist electoral cooperation in the 1964 and 1966 elections. See Chapter Five.

communal services (including those performed by both the provincial and municipal administrations) has increased dramatically. From 40 million crowns in 1874, total communal expenditures and investments rose to nearly 15 billion crowns in 1964. As a percentage of Sweden's gross national product, communal expenditures grew from 3.2 percent to 15.3 percent during the same period, thereby exceeding the share of national government expenditures which was 12.5 percent of the GNP in 1964.[9]

Local government concentrates nearly three quarters of its resources in three areas: primary and secondary education, health care, and social welfare. (See Table 6.) Between 1950 and 1964 communal investments in welfare services increased nearly 225 percent; the growth in health and education programs was 169 and 147 percent, respectively.[10]

In addition to their service functions, provincial and municipal government structures play a variety of important supportive roles in the formation of national policies. Election to local office often provides aspiring parliamentarians their initial legislative experience, and even after a successful campaign for parliament most members of the Riksdag simultaneously retain positions in *landsting* or local assemblies. In 1965 nearly 72 percent of the deputies in the lower house were active in provincial and/or municipal politics compared to 68 percent of those in the upper house. In both cases over half of the delegates served in municipal

Table 6   Communal Consumption, 1954–1963[a]

Area	Crowns (in millions)			Percentage		
	1954	1960	1963	1954	1960	1963
Education	1060	1817	2510	34.5	34.6	34.1
Health Care and Hospitals	829	1440	2051	26.9	27.5	27.9
Social Welfare	345	508	741	11.2	9.7	10.1
Courts and Police	183	291	400	5.9	5.5	5.4
Churches	188	279	354	6.1	5.3	4.8
Road Construction	120	229	290	3.9	4.4	3.9
Administration	234	497	761	7.6	9.5	10.3
Miscellaneous[b]	119	182	257	3.9	3.5	3.5
Total	3078	5243	7364	100.0	100.0	100.0

[a]Sweden, Justitiedepartmentet, *Statens offentliga utredningar 1965: 54, Författningsfrågan och det kommunala sambandet* (Stockholm: Justitiedepartementet, 1965), p. 42.

[b]Includes fire protection and sanitation.

9 *SOU 1965:54*, p. 41.
10 *SOU 1965:54*, p. 42.

councils while just under half held office in a provincial *landsting* or administration. (See Table 7.)

Such personal unions between local and national politics allow communal representatives a direct opportunity to participate in Riksdag deliberations affecting local government functions and organization. Conversely, of course, individual deputies are able to interpret and administer such policies in their dual role as provincial or municipal officials. One result is that experimental projects or reforms in one district may serve as a model for subsequent Riksdag legislation applying to the entire nation.

Until constitutional reforms introducing unicameralism went into effect on January 1, 1971, thereby abolishing the upper house of the Swedish parliament, the provincial assemblies contributed an additional support for the Riksdag through their function as electoral colleges. By enabling the *landsting* and urban provincial districts to elect fully 40 percent of the total parliamentary membership, indirect elections accorded provincial government a major institutional link with the national political system. This did not mean that the provinces exercised influence on parliamentary decisions as *provinces*. In practice indirect elections served primarily as an additional channel of *party* representation in the Riksdag.

Table 7   Members of Parliament Active in Local Politics, 1965[a]

Chamber	Total Membership	Total MPs Active in Local Politics	
		Number	Percentage
Lower House	230	167	71.7
Upper House	151	103	68.2

Chamber	Total Membership	MPs Holding Office in			
		Municipal Assemblies		Provincial Assemblies	
		Number	Percentage	Number	Percentage
Lower House	230	135	57.9	100	42.9
Upper House	151	84	55.6	67	44.4

[a]Adapted from Sweden, Justitiedepartmentet, *Statens offentliga utredningar 1965: 54, Författningsfrågan och det kommunala sambandet*, pp. 572–573.

STYLE OF COMMUNAL POLITICS

Underlying the successive expansion of communal services in recent decades is elite consensus on the intrinsic value of local structures as decentralized instruments of policy implementation, political participation, and self-government. For reasons of tradition as well as administrative expediency, party leaders of all partisan persuasion have repeatedly affirmed the importance of local government as a fundamental component of pluralist democracy in Sweden.

Among provincial and municipal officials themselves, common attitudes of compromise and pragmatism, described as general elite attributes in the preceding chapter, are particularly pronounced. Because most substantive policy decisions affecting provincial-municipal functions are made by national authorities, the stakes of political competition on the local level are relatively minimal. This encourages a high degree of nonpartisanship as the dominant style of communal politics.

An important illustration of nonpartisanship in regional-local politics is the pattern of appointments to provincial governorships. As Table 8 indicates, the executive appointed 49 governors from 1945 to 1965. More Social Democrats were named provincial governors than members of any other single party, but significantly the largest group—nearly half of the total—comprised civil servants or nonpartisans.

Within the provincial and municipal assemblies, plural executives provide a major institutional incentive for policy collaboration among local party leaders. Members of the executive

Table 8 Appointment of Provincial Governors,
1945–1965[a]

Classifications	Total
Civil servants or nonpartisans[b]	24
Social Democrats	13
Liberals	6
Conservatives	4
Center	2
Total	49

[a]My computations from *Sveriges statskalender* (Stockholm: Almqvist & Wiksell, 1945–1965).
[b]Nonpartisans include those who were employed or in private industry for whom no party membership was cited in the Swedish Who's Who (*Vem är det*).

committees in the various *landsting* and rural-urban assemblies are elected by proportional representation. Hence, in contrast to the principle of majority rule in the Riksdag, permanent all-party coalitions characterize most provincial and municipal executive bodies.

A functional necessity for permanent provincial-local party coalitions is provided by the checkerboard distribution of regional party strength. No party has consistently dominated provincial elections; the Social Democrats have won a national plurality in three postwar elections (1946, 1950, and 1962), while the non-socialist bloc has also received a relative majority in three elections (1954, 1958, and 1966). Only once has a single party—the Social Democrats—won an absolute majority in a provincial election. (See Table 9.)

A similar pattern prevails at the municipal level. In the 1966 communal election, for example, a single party amassed a majority in only 224 out of Sweden's 900 rural-urban communes. Of this total the Social Democrats won a majority in 171 local districts, the Center party in 50, the Liberals in 2, and the Conservatives in 1.

The absence of clearly defined partisan majorities in most provincial and municipal elections combined with provisions for plural executives thus contributes to the pervasiveness of Sweden's characteristic nonpartisan style of local politics. Although individual political spokesmen have intermittently advocated the substitution of communal parliamentarism for the present system of permanent coalitions, especially in communes where there is a persistent Socialist or nonsocialist majority, no concerted move has been made to abandon the prevailing emphasis on interparty compromise in communal affairs. Issues are occasionally debated along party lines, for example, the nomination of a local chief

Table 9   Postwar Communal Elections:
Nonsocialist bloc and social democratic percentages

Year	Nonsocialist Bloc	Social Democrats
1946	43.3	48.6
1950	46.3	48.6
1954	47.7	47.4
1958	49.1	46.8
1962	45.7	50.5
1966	49.4	42.2

magistrate, but this appears to be the exception rather than the rule. Instead, the major criterion in deciding most local questions is technical expediency rather than partisan commitment.

THE LIMITS OF CONSENSUS

Despite the characteristic pattern of nonpartisan behavior among political actors in the provincial and municipal assemblies, it does not follow that local government is entirely immune from political controversy. On the contrary, partisan differences have generated extensive debate on the functions and role of local government. In light of the centralizing tendencies wrought by factors of legal and political coordination at the apex of the Swedish system, however, the principal forum for such debate is the national level of politics rather than the communal level.

The limits of consensus concerning local politics in Sweden have been revealed in a succession of policy disputes among the established parties. The tension between contradictory priorities of collectivism and individualism among members of the Swedish elite has sustained partisan cleavages on specific communal policies as well as the communal link itself.

Three examples of partisan cleavage stand out as particularly significant: the extension of welfare services, housing policies, and the effect of parliamentary reform on local government. In each case consensus on general principles of policy has been qualified by conflicting party claims advanced on behalf of special ideological and/or tactical considerations.

At issue in recurrent conflicts over welfare and housing, as illustrations of substantive policy disagreements, is not local government per se, but rather efforts to establish guidelines for the functions that national legislation requires communal authorities to administer.

In the case of welfare services, Socialist initiatives have led in the postwar period to a significant expansion of basic programs designed to equalize economic and social opportunities. Nonsocialist leaders have responded to the extension of welfare provisions by endorsing the need for collective guarantees of individual security, but they have sought to modify particular policy proposals with counterarguments against what they perceive as excessive detailed regulation from above. The Conservatives especially have resisted centralized responsibility for welfare services by advocating tax reductions that, in their view, would allow greater incentives, for example, through increased personal savings and investments, for *individuals* to maximize their own potential for economic security. To achieve this goal the Conservatives advocated during the 1960 electoral campaign that state allowances for the first child be abolished as a means to reduce government expenditures and taxes—a proposal that may have accounted in large measure for the Conservative loss of six seats in that election.

Similarly, conflict between collectivist and individualist policy perspectives is discernible in the party debate on housing legislation. As a result largely of Socialist efforts to achieve equitable living conditions for all citizens, Sweden's housing market has been progressively brought under direct government supervision in recent decades. Nationwide rent controls were imposed in 1942, and the state—acting through the municipalities—has subsequently assumed primary responsibility for the construction of new apartments and houses. By redoubling their own building efforts and channeling a significant share of government loans to cooperative associations, national and municipal authorities have increased the number of dwelling units constructed under direct or indirect state auspices from 48.8 percent of all new apartments and houses completed in 1949 to 63.8 percent in 1967.

The municipalization of Sweden's housing market, however, has not achieved its anticipated results. Because of continuing urbanization, industrial concentration in or near the larger cities, and increased demand for better living facilities, Sweden—like the other Scandinavian states—has experienced a severe housing shortage during the postwar period. In attempting to meet this need, communal authorities have undertaken extraordinary steps to stimulate the construction of new housing units—with objectively impressive results. By the early 1960s Sweden was building the second highest number of housing units in relation to its population of any country in the world—9.9 units per 1000 population, compared to 10.1 to 1000 in West Germany, the highest ranking nation—with 40 percent of all Swedes living in apartments or homes that have been built since the end of World War II.[11] During the rest of the decade the ratio grew even higher, reaching 12.8 by 1967. In aggregate terms Sweden constructed

[11] Ernst Michanek, *Für und gegen den Wohlfahrtstaat* (Stockholm: The Swedish Institute, 1964), p. 19.

between 1962 and 1967 an annual average of nearly 91,000 new dwellings. Of this total, 63.8 percent was in the form of apartments.[12]

Yet the housing shortage persists. According to government statistics, 215,157 apartments or houses, out of 2,582,151 dwellings that were occupied in 1965, are overcrowded.[13] Nonsocialist spokesmen claim that more than 463,000 persons have registered with municipal authorities to obtain a new residence, with 158,000 lacking their own place to live and the remainder seeking to move to larger quarters or another city.[14] Often the waiting period for a new apartment in Stockholm is six to eight years.

Thus providing a tangible basis for opposition criticism of the government's inability to resolve an important domestic issue, Sweden's housing shortage has prompted a series of nonsocialist attacks on communal construction policies. Specifically, nonsocialist leaders have criticized Socialist-sponsored guidelines on rent controls and the use of government loans for construction purposes. While not renouncing communal responsibility to help provide adequate housing, spokesmen of the Center, Liberal, and Conservative parties would delegate greater authority for housing construction to private interests. Thus they jointly advocate, as an alternative to the Socialist emphasis on collective action, an easing of credit restrictions for private builders and more concerted efforts by the government to relieve pressures of urbanization by supporting the localization of industry in less populated districts.

DEBATE ON THE COMMUNAL LINK

The third major area of partisan controversy over the role of local government—the communal link with national politics—grew out of a common commitment among the established parties to rationalize Sweden's parliamentary system. Recognizing that the formal Swedish constitution, adopted in 1809, failed to incorporate many important principles of the "living construction" such as unwritten traditions of cabinet supremacy and parliament responsibility, the national cabinet appointed a Royal Commission in 1954 to "undertake a modernization of [the Swedish] constitu-

---

[12] Percentages calculated from *Statistisk årsbok 1968*, pp. 222–223.

[13] Nordic Council, *Yearbook of Nordic Statistics* (Stockholm: Nordic Council, 1969), p. 69.

[14] Centerpartiet och folkpartiet, *Mittensamverkan 68* (Stockholm: Bokförlaget Folk & Samhälle, 1968), p. 59.

tion . . . from the perspective of the functional problems of democracy."[15] When the commission submitted its final report in 1963 recommending broad changes in political structures and practices, an intensive partisan debate ensued that ultimately led to a basic redefinition of local-national relations.

According to the terms of reference issued by the Department of Justice, the Royal Commission was directed to examine possible changes in the electoral law; the possibilities of extending the use of national referenda; ministerial functions and cabinet responsibility; the codification of civil liberties; and the structure of the Riksdag.[16] Deliberations extended 9 years, and only after 30 versions of a revised constitution had been rejected did the delegates succeed in attaining general consensus on most of the topics assigned them for consideration.[17] Even so they failed to agree on what proved to be the most controversial subject of the later political debate on their report: the issue of parliamentary reform. A majority of six members favored the creation of a unicameral legislature, while two members recommended the retention of the bicameral structure that had been created in the constitutional reforms of 1865–1866.

After the commission report was published in May 1963, leaders of the established parties responded by endorsing the commission's recommendations to incorporate parliamentarism into the Swedish constitution and to rationalize parliamentary procedures. But like members of the commission, albeit for different reasons, they diverged in their attitudes toward reforming the structure of the Riksdag. Ultimately they agreed on the introduction of unicameralism, but until that decision was reached Socialist and nonsocialist forces confronted each other in a major conflict of principle.

The focus of debate was the prevailing system of indirect elections to the upper house. Throughout the twentieth century the different procedures that were used in the election of the lower and upper house deputies had led to significant discrepancies in the composition of the two chambers. Shifts in public opinion were immediately discernible in the lower house due to the direct election of all members simultaneously. Staggered individual terms of eight years and indirect elections meant, however, a much more

[15] Sweden, Justitiedepartementet, *Statens offentliga utredningar 1963:16, Författningsutredningen: VI, Sveriges statsskick. Del 1. Lagförslag* (Stockholm: Justitiedepartementet, 1963), p. 5. Hereafter referred to as *SOU 1963:16.*

[16] *SOU 1963:16,* p. 9.

[17] *Dagens Nyheter,* January 27, 1964, p. 11.

gradual turnover of membership in the first chamber. As the mandate of representatives chosen in the fourth year of a provincial assembly's term did not expire until 12 years after the communal election to which they owed their seats, there was, in fact, an average lag of 6 years between a given communal election and changes in the composition of the upper chamber. The political implication of delayed membership turnover was that the upper house could serve as "a conservative safeguard . . . [for] the power of a party that [had] been in power for some time."[18] Conversely, the fact that a party or parties scored electoral gains in a communal election did not become apparent in the Riksdag until after a lapse of several years.

Originally instituted in the nineteenth century as a mechanism to protect oligarchical interests, indirect elections had become by the middle of the twentieth century a principal means for the Social Democrats to maintain their control of cabinet office. Despite the absence of clear majorities in postwar communal elections (except for the Socialist victory in 1962), every communal election since 1950 had nevertheless resulted in an increase in Socialist strength in relation to the party's support in intervening elections to the lower house. In conjunction with wartime Socialist victories in communal elections, the post-1950 advances had enabled the Social Democrats to maintain a majority of seats in the upper chamber that effectively compensated for their minority status from 1952 to 1960 in the lower house.[19] When the two chambers voted together in crucial "joint votes" on financial matters, the Socialists had thus been able to command a majority of the combined parliamentary membership and, as a result, retain executive leadership.

Socialist leaders could therefore view the proposed abolition of the upper house and indirect elections, which the majority report of the Royal Commission on constitutional reform had recommended, with somewhat less equanimity than nonsocialist spokesmen. From the Socialist point of view the introduction of unicameralism and the simultaneous direct election of all members of parliament could mean the rise of a nonsocialist government to power should the opposition parties once again receive a popular majority (as they had in 1952). For precisely that reason, nonsocialist leaders could be expected to favor unicameralism and an end to indirect elections.

---

[18] Nils Andrén, *Modern Swedish Government* (Stockholm: Almqvist & Wiksell, 1961), p. 42.
[19] See Chapter Seven.

The initial response of the governing Social Democrats to the Royal Commission's report was to propose a partial parliamentary reform in which the first chamber would be dissolved after the 1966 communal election. The entire membership of the upper house would then be reelected to eliminate the delayed effects of previous communal elections its composition. Nonsocialist leaders rejected this proposal on the grounds "that a partial reform of this sort should hardly be implemented when a basic . . . constitutional reform is so close at hand."[19] Two months later the chairmen of the Socialist and the three nonsocialist parties met in an attempt to reach a general agreement on the broader issues of electoral and parliamentary revision. When they failed to achieve a compromise, the principal lines of dissent dividing the two blocs became clear.

Having abandoned their earlier suggestion for a provisional reform of the first chamber in the face of united nonsocialist opposition, the Socialists asserted their new policy initiative: the retention of a communal electoral link between the provinces and the Riksdag. Prime Minister Erlander stated, in a preliminary explanation of his party's position, that "a connection between communal and national policies . . ." was an "absolute condition" for a constitutional settlement.[20] Citing the complementary tasks performed by national administrative boards and communal authorities in such fields as welfare, housing, and education, Erlander declared: "One of the reasons why Swedish democracy functions well is that communal policies play such an important role in social affairs."[21] Thus the Social Democrats concluded that some sort of guarantee must be provided to maintain effective provincial ties with the national parliament under the new constitution. Erlander defined three possible means to achieve this end: preservation of the bicameral system with minor modifications, creation of a unicameral legislature with a third of its membership chosen indirectly by the provincial assemblies, or the simultaneous election of deputies to the Riksdag and the provincial assemblies.[22]

Tactically each of the alternatives that the Socialist chairman proposed as a possible basis for constitutional agreement would tend to retain the advantages enjoyed by the majority party under then prevailing conditions. Modified bicameralism would simply perpetuate the existing structure, while the indirect election of a

[20] Statement by Center party chairman Gunnar Hedlund, quoted in *Dagens Nyheter*, January 14, 1964, p. 9.
[21] *Dagens Nyheter*, March 18, 1964, p. 16.
[22] *Dagens Nyheter*, March 18, 1964, p. 16.

third of the deputies in a unicameral Riksdag would constitute an approximation of the bicameral system with its concomitant implications for successive renewal. The simultaneous election of representatives to provincial assemblies and the national parliament would preserve electoral identification of popular local welfare services with Riksdag policies, presumably to the benefit of the Social Democrats.

The response of the three nonsocialist parties to Erlander's pronouncement proved equally determined by partisan considerations. Because indirect elections or the retention of the bicameral system would countermand the potential advantages that the nonsocialist parties hoped to gain under unicameralism, all three nonsocialist chairmen were sharply critical of the Socialist "ultimatum" to maintain a communal link between the provincial assemblies and the composition of the Riksdag. Asserting that "communal questions would be threatened with submersion in national political propaganda" if indirect elections were retained under unicameralism, the Conservative chairman, Gunnar Heckscher, reaffirmed his party's endorsement of a unicameral Riksdag whose members would be chosen simultaneously by popular mandate.[23] In a parallel statement the chairman of the Liberal party, Bertil Ohlin, maintained that "the electorate should have the opportunity to determine the composition of the Riksdag and the nation's government in a single election."[24]

Subsequent elaboration of party viewpoints confirmed the fundamental cleavage separating the Social Democrats and the nonsocialist parties in their respective assessments of the implications of constitutional reform. At the party's twenty-second congress in June 1964, Socialist delegates endorsed a motion submitted by Erlander that a "close association between communal and national policies is a requisite for a . . . progressive reform policy."[25] Concurrently, each of the nonsocialist parties formally sanctioned unicameralism. Delegates to the Liberal party convention voted on June 7, 1964, that elections to a single-chamber parliament should be simultaneous and direct, while a similar motion was adopted by the Conservatives during their congress the following week. On June 16 the Center party adopted an eight-

23 *Dagens Nyheter*, March 18, 1964, p. 16.

24 *Dagens Nyheter*, March 18, 1964, p. 16.

25 The motion was adopted by acclamation on June 10, 1964. Sveriges socialdemokratiska arbetareparti, *Socialdemokratiska arbetarepartiets 22:e kongress 1964. Protokoll* (Stockholm: Tiden, 1964), p. 417. Hereafter referred to as *Protokoll*.

point program on constitutional reform calling, among other things, for a unicameral legislature "chosen in *direct vote* in a single election."[26]

Conflicting attitudes toward the issue of indirect elections dominated the constitutional debate during the 1964 electoral campaign. In a series of television and radio duels, Socialist and nonsocialist spokesmen reiterated earlier party viewpoints on the retention of some form of communal link in a future Riksdag and the necessity for direct parliamentary elections, respectively. The impasse between Socialist and nonsocialist forces was tentatively resolved only after the September election. In a major policy declaration in the lower house on November 12, 1964, Erlander asserted Socialist willingness to resume consultations with opposition leaders in an effort to achieve a compromise solution. The nonsocialist parties subsequently agreed to the appointment of a new Royal Commission to consider the issues of a communal link in connection with a general reappraisal of communal democracy.

The Royal Commission, composed of two Social Democrats, one representative from each of the three nonsocialist parties, and two civil servants, began consultations in the spring of 1965. Its recommendations, published in September 1965, simply reiterated previous party positions.[27] A majority report endorsed by the Social Democrats on the commission concluded that "it is necessary in devising a new constitution to find a means of retaining the electoral link between the Riksdag and communal administration."[28] The three nonsocialist members dissented in a formal reservation, arguing that the majority's insistence on the necessity to retain such a link missed the point of constitutional reform, namely that "the Swedish people, like many other people in the Western democracies, . . . should have the opportunity *in a single election* to determine *directly* the entire composition of the Riksdag."[29]

Eight months later, in April 1966, the cabinet once again appointed a Royal Commission to continue deliberations on the constitutional reform question. In the midst of its deliberations, the decisive event occurred that finally ended the constitutional impasse: the September 1966 communal election. Suffering a decisive defeat, the Social Democrats fell to their lowest point in

---

[26] Stockholm newspapers, June 17, 1964.
[27] *SOU 1965:54.*
[28] *SOU 1965:54*, p. 105.
[29] *SOU 1965:54*, p. 108. Italics in the original.

electoral support in over three decades (42.2 percent of the total). The opposition parties, campaigning as a broadly united nonsocialist bloc, received in contrast their highest percentage of the national vote since 1958 (49.4 percent). As one consequence of the election's outcome, both sides to the constitutional conflict resolved to reach a compromise on the issue of a communal link. Privately conceding that their loss reflected, in part, a repudiation of their attempts to restrict direct elections to future parliaments, the Social Democrats dropped their earlier proposals for the retention of either a modified bicameral system or indirect elections to a unicameral Riksdag. Encouraged that the election had revealed an unanticipated popular response to their own communal policies, nonsocialist spokesmen concluded that some form of electoral link between local and national politics would not be entirely to their disadvantage.

Thus leaders of the Social Democratic and three opposition parties concurred in March 1967 on the introduction of unicameralism, with direct elections to parliament to take place at the same time as elections to the municipal and provincial assemblies. This agreement was formally codified in the final report of the third Royal Commission, which was issued in April 1967.[30] Following ratification by parliament in 1967 and 1969, the four-party compromise was implemented in January 1971. The first elections to Sweden's new unicameral Riksdag, which brought to an end the previous system of indirect elections by members of the provincial assemblies, were held in September 1970.

LOCAL GOVERNMENT: FUTURE PROSPECTS

The course of the constitutional struggle over the communal link provides instructive insights into the balance between opposing elite attitudes in Sweden. Seeking to maintain cabinet offices as a necessary condition for the further extension of collective influence on the nation's economic and social system, the Social Democrats viewed a communal electoral link as an appropriate means to help secure their base of parliamentary support. In response nonsocialist leaders endorsed unicameralism and direct elections as essential guarantees against the potential abuse of political power by a single political party.

---

[30] Sweden, Justitiedepartementet, *Statens offentliga utredningar 1967:26, Partiell författningsreform* (Stockholm: Justitiedepartementet, 1967).

Ultimately, the divergent attitudes between Socialist and nonsocialist spokesmen did not preclude a compromise solution. On the contrary, the Social Democrats had insisted throughout the party debate on the communal link that a common agreement among the four democratic parties was necessary.[31] As during the historical struggles that accompanied Sweden's political and social modernization, the outcome of the 1964–1967 constitutional controversy demonstrated that elite dualisms are mitigated by a shared inclination among antagonists to settle their differences through mutual accommodation.

In the specific context of communal politics, the issue of the communal link is the only one of the three areas of interparty conflict discussed above to be presently "solved." By their very nature, welfare and housing policies will continue to provoke electoral competition and ideological cleavages among Sweden's political representatives. Having assumed significantly expanded functions as an instrument of an increasingly complex welfare state, local government will remain an important object of political controversy.

[31] At the Socialist party congress in June 1964, delegates affirmed that a constitutional revision "should be endorsed by the greatest possible unity among the various political movements." *Protokoll*, p. 417.

FIVE
A MULTIPARTY SYSTEM IN TRANSITION
The dialectics of party change

Within the limits imposed by prevailing elite consensus on basic political values and beliefs, the radical debate of the 1960s produced by the end of the decade significant if indirect effects on the internal characteristics of parties as well as interest organizations in Sweden. The radical liberal and New Left activists have by no means succeeded in revolutionizing domestic structures, but their demands for political and economic reforms contributed nonetheless to long-term processes of change in group relations. The most important political consequence of such change is the incipient transformation of the multiparty system.

THE SWEDISH PARTY SYSTEM: GENERAL CHARACTERISTICS

Outwardly the Swedish party system is characterized by its multiplicity of parties. A factor that has helped perpetuate multiplicity is the use of proportional representation in elections to the Riksdag and local government assemblies. For the election of 310 deputies to parliament Sweden is divided into 28 constituencies; an average of eleven representatives is selected in each. An additional 40 representatives are chosen from national ballots in which the entire nation serves as a single constituency. All citizens over 20 years old are eligible to vote under a national system of permanent registration. Voting is by the list system, with district and local party organizations determining nominations. Originally based on the d'Hondt formula of proportional representation, Sweden's electoral system was changed in 1952 when a modified version of the Sainte Lagüe method was adopted, which utilizes uneven numbers (1.4, 5, 7, etc.) to calculate comparison figures and, derivately, the number of seats that is allowed each of the parties.[1] The effect of both systems has been to lessen incentives for the consolidation of parties and to accord parties receiving 10 percent or more of the popular vote a slight overrepresentation at the expense of smaller ones. A new barrier to small parties was introduced in the constitutional reform of 1967–1969, which became effective in the September 1970 election, in the form of provisions similar to the 5 percent clause in the West German electoral law.[2] A party must now receive either 4 percent of the national vote or 12 percent of the votes cast in a single constituency to be apportioned seats in the Riksdag.

On a conventional left-right continuum, the principal parties in Sweden are the Left Party-Communists, the Social Democrats, the Center, the Liberals, and the Moderate Unity party. Each displays a high degree of internal cohesion, which is sustained by well-integrated bureaucratic structures and partisan loyalty among members. The parties are organized along similar lines, with each hierarchy consisting of local and district associations, national

[1] Under the d'Hondt system, the total of the votes for each party in a given district is divided successively by the cardinal numbers (1, 2, 3, and so forth) and seats are awarded to the highest quotients obtained, thus ensuring maximum proportionality. An important feature of its application in Sweden was that parties were permitted to form electoral cartels, that is, pool their strength to take advantage of "surplus votes" that otherwise would have been lost if seats were apportioned solely according to the individual party totals. The nonsocialist parties had utilized the cartel system extensively after 1928. A principal reason for its abolition when the Lagüe formula was adopted in 1952 was the Center party's agreement the previous year to join the Socialists in a coalition ministry, a step that made the previous practice of local alliances between the Center and the Conservatives or Liberals politically awkward. The Lagüe method was partly intended to compensate the Center for its anticipated loss of surplus votes in individual constituencies. Nothing in the new electoral law, however, would prohibit parties from sponsoring a common list of candidates. For more detailed discussions of Swedish electoral law see Dankwart A. Rustow, *The Politics of Compromise*, (Princeton, N.J.: Princeton University Press, 1955), pp. 123–128, and Nils Andrén, *Modern Swedish Government* (Stockholm: Almqvist & Wiksell, 1961), pp. 69–89.

[2] In postwar elections the 5 percent barrier has effectively excluded a number of splinter parties, ranging from the Communists to the right-wing National Democratic party, from the West German Bundestag. See Gerhard Loewenberg, *Parliament in the German Political System* (Ithaca, N.Y.: Cornell University Press, 1967), pp. 66–67.

committees, and small executive committees made up of from 17 to 45 members. Complementing the formal party organizations are auxiliary youth, student, and women's associations.[3]

The highest policy organ in all five parties is nominally the party congress, which is a representative body elected by members on the district level. Most of the party congresses convene at two or three year intervals, while that of the Center party meets annually. Delegates to the national congresses debate party objectives, consider motions submitted by the leadership and individual members, and formally elect the party chairmen. In reality, however, the parliamentary leaders—acting through the various executive committees—exert the decisive influence in shaping party policy.[4]

Discipline among parliamentary deputies is enforced by "strong moral pressure" and potential collective sanctions.[5] The ultimate sanction is that a party may refuse to renominate a member who has overtly challenged the party leadership in important legislation. Because the parties exercise a monopoly over nomination procedures, much as in Britain and in most other Western European nations, no candidate in Sweden can hope to compete successfully for office without a party's endorsement.[6]

To finance their activities, the parties have traditionally derived their income from membership dues and contributions from individuals and interest groups. Since 1966 the parties have also received official subsidies from the national government. State support was endorsed by the Riksdag in 1965 ostensibly to help subsidize party-affiliated newspapers. Public funds are allocated according to the average number of votes each party receives in two successive national elections.[7]

---

[3] Membership totals of the various women's and youth associations are given in Table 4 on p. 58.

[4] Pär-Erik Back, "Det svenska partiväsendet," in Arthur Thomson (ed.), *Samhälle och riksdag*, II (Stockholm: Almqvist & Wiksell, 1966), pp. 40–55.

[5] Back, "Det svenska partiväsendet," pp. 132–138.

[6] An exception occurred in 1968 when five deputies were elected to parliament as candidates of nonsocialist electoral alliances in southern Sweden, but they ran for office with local party support and not as independents. Once in the Riksdag, the MPs joined the parliamentary groups of the established national parties. The most recent example of party discipline being invoked to expel a disloyal member was the dismissal of a Liberal deputy who had abstained in a crucial parliamentary vote on supplementary pensions in 1959. See p. 222.

[7] Nils Andrén, "Sweden: State Support for Political Parties," *Scandinavian Political Studies*, 3 (New York: Columbia University Press, 1968), pp. 221–229. On the basis of calculations in *Dagens Nyheter*, Andrén reports on p. 229 the following sources of party income in 1967:

Figure 1   Patterns of Party Concentration

Degree of Party Cohesion	Two-Party Systems	Multiparty Systems
High	Britain	Sweden, Norway, Denmark, Netherlands
Low	United States	France, Italy

According to Dahl's classification of political parties, the Swedish system therefore exemplifies dispersed concentration *among* parties but relatively high unity *within* parties.[8] These salient features of Sweden's multiparty system, which are shared by Norway and Denmark as well as several continental countries such as the Netherlands and Luxembourg, provide a distinctive contrast to party systems with either a greater concentration of numbers and/or less internal cohesion. (See Figure 1.)

The multiplicity of parties in Sweden, however, constitutes a largely surface expression of more fundamental characteristics of the party system. Despite its fragmentation among five parties, the Swedish party system consists in reality of a tripartite cleavage that cuts across at least some of the established party boundaries. Comparable to similar patterns of party cleavage in Norway and Denmark, the three principal party groupings in Sweden include the New Left (organized as the Left Party-Communists), the Social Democrats, and the nonsocialist bloc (encompassing the Center, the Liberals, and the Moderate Unity party).[9] In actual political—especially parliamentary—behavior, Sweden's political divi-

	Sources of Income (Crowns)			
Party	*Membership Fees*	*State Support*	*Other Income*	*Total Income*
Moderate Unity	600,000	3,540,000	5,100,000	9,240,000
Center	342,300	3,423,000	485,000	4,250,300
Liberals	202,200	4,245,000	2,479,000	6,926,200
Social Democrats	2,100,000	11,520,000	5,992,000	19,623,000
Left Party—Communists	150,000	645,000	640,000	1,435,000

[8] Robert A. Dahl, "Patterns of Opposition," in Dahl (ed.), *Political Oppositions in Western Democracies* (New Haven, Conn.: Yale University Press, 1966), pp. 332–336.

[9] In both Norway and Denmark, as noted in Chapter One, the nonsocialist parties have united on common programs to form coalition governments. An internal dispute concerning the pending issues of Norway's admission to the Common Market caused the resignation of the Norwegian coalition on March 1, 1971.

sion has on occasion coalesced into an even more simplified Socialist versus nonsocialist alignment.

The tripartite political cleavage in Sweden reflects disparate ideological orientations among party spokesmen toward collectivist-individualist assumptions concerning the goals of political action (discussed in Chapter Three) and differing attitudes toward system change. The theoretical range of these dual party characteristics, based on the concept of modernization presented in the introduction to this volume, is presented schematically in Figure 2. In the case of parties in Sweden, both the Social Democrats and the Left Party-Communists may be classified as collectivist, although they differ significantly in their respective prescriptions for desirable collective measures. In contrast the three nonsocialist parties manifest a common bloc identity, despite differences in policy priorities and electoral clientele, that rests on shared ideological assumptions affirming an individualist theory of political action. A continuing process of response and counterresponse among these three party groupings accounts for shifts in political attitudes toward system change.

As a review of party developments and programs reveals, all of the parties in Sweden have changed over time along both dimensions of party characteristics. The success of particular measures initiated by the Social Democrats, the erosion of traditional sources of electoral support, and the resurgence of ideological controversy in the 1960s have combined to transform the parties as well as the party system itself.

THE SOCIAL DEMOCRATS

From its inception as a mass-based collectivist movement dedicated to the radical transformation of Sweden's socioeconomic and political system, the Social Democratic party has pursued a gradualist program of change rather than ideological dogmatism.

Figure 2 Party Characteristics: Orientations toward Ideology and Change

Ideological Basis	Attitude Toward System Change		
	Regressive Change	Maintaining Change	Transforming Change
Collectivist			
Individualist			

Theoretically the Socialists advocate the reorganization of Swedish society "so that the right to determine production and distribution is placed in the hands of all the people, citizens are freed from their dependence on all types of power groups beyond their control, and a social order composed of classes is replaced by a community of persons cooperating together on the basis of freedom and quality."[10] In practice, this Socialist vision of economic democracy and a classless society has been qualified by a traditional willingness among party leaders to work within the established pluralist framework, seeking close cooperation with both the nonsocialist parties in parliament and private enterprise outside the formal structures of government.

An important first step toward ideological moderation in promoting long-range goals of radical reform was taken in 1889 with the party's decision not to initiate violence as an instrument of political change. Delegates at the founding congress resolved that

> Sweden's Social Democratic Party—in its efforts to organize the Swedish working class for its conquest of political power—will make use of such means that correspond to the people's natural sense of justice. The contemporary program which we have formulated and for which we are working is the best proof that we, for our part, are by no means striving for a violent revolution. The Congress expressly refutes the foolish plans which are accredited to us by our enemies that we wish to endanger the entire labor movement by attempting some sort of violent coup without sufficient support by the people. . . . Revolutions can never be "made"; but should the blindness of egoism among the ruling circles provoke a violent revolution in desperate self-defense, our place is assigned and we are prepared to do all that is necessary to help the people secure and preserve as valuable fruits of the battle as possible.[11]

The implications of the resolution, Rustow observes, are clear. The Socialists "did not repudiate violence as a means of attaining political power: the time might come when it would take part in a political revolt. But the party would not take such a step without the spontaneous support of the masses."[12]

Attitudes favoring moderation inspired the party's simultaneous decision on its relations with other parties in Sweden. Like

[10] Hans Wieslander (ed.), *De politiska partiernas program* (Stockholm: Bokförlaget Prisma, 1964), p. 107.

[11] Herbert Tingsten, *Den svenska socialdemokratiens idéutveckling*, I (Stockholm: Tiden, 1941), pp. 21–22.

[12] Rustow, *The Politics of Compromise*, pp. 50–51.

Social Democratic parties elsewhere in the late nineteenth-century Europe, the Swedish Socialists confronted a choice between cooperating with nonsocialist forces to promote common objectives or retaining ideological purity by refusing such alliances from above. As stated by H. Hilding Nordström, the dilemma was whether "the party should from the beginning assume . . . a purely negative standpoint and reject all associations with what the Gotha program called the 'single reactionary mass'. . . . Or should the party seek an intermediate course of action that . . . would allow it scope to support reforms within the framework of existing society which would benefit members of the working class?"[13]

In choosing the second alternative, party delegates at the founding congress responded to Branting's appeal for moderation. Because the Social Democratic movement was far too small in 1889 to initiate revolutionary change on its own resources, the only possibility for the newly formed party to exert immediate political influence was through a tactical alliance with the growing liberal forces. As Branting had written in the Socialist theoretical journal, *Tiden*: " 'even though [the Socialists'] social program differs from that of the Liberals, their political demands are largely the same.' "[14] Hence the congress majority resolved that the party may "determine for the time being which of these groups indicating a serious willingness to defend and extend the rights of the people [it may work with] in common efforts in elections, agitation for the right to vote, and other points."[15]

Having foresworn unprovoked violence and affirmed cooperation with the Liberals in a joint struggle for universal suffrage, the Swedish Socialists thus made a decisive break with fundamental principles of orthodox Marxism. The trend toward ideological revisionism became even more pronounced in subsequent decades. Lasalle's theory of the "iron law of wages," which stated that capitalists kept wages as low as possible consistent with the minimal subsistence of the workers, was dropped from the 1897 program, and henceforth only ritualistic attention was paid to the traditional Socialist demand to nationalize industry. Even more importantly, the party resolved to support parliamentary government and piecemeal reform efforts.

Ideological pragmatism enabled the Social Democrats to extend their electoral following beyond the confines of narrow group interests. With rapid industrialization broadening the numerical

---

[13] H. Hilding Nordström, *Sveriges socialdemokratiska arbetareparti under genomsbrottsåren, 1889–1894* (Stockholm: KF, 1938), p. 124.

[14] Quoted in Nordström, p. 124.

[15] Nordström, p. 130.

basis of working-class support for the party after the turn of the century, the Social Democrats became the largest party in the lower house of parliament in 1914. Subsequent electoral advances were attributed not only to continued industrialization but, given the mixed economy of most of Sweden's rural districts, also to the party's success in aggregating agrarian interests. At the same time the Social Democrats made significant inroads in the middle-class by advocating comprehensive measures to sustain economic growth and insure social justice and welfare. As a result of their broadly based appeal, the Socialists have consistently amassed a third or more of the popular vote since 1922. In five elections they have won over 50 percent of the national vote (1938, 1940, 1942, 1962, and 1968). (See Table 10.)

The personalities of successive Socialist chairmen proved a major factor in sustaining the party's gradualist strategy of reform. Branting's behavior as an ardent advocate of ideological pragmatism and conciliation toward other groups in society served as a model for the leadership style of each of his successors: Per Albin Hansson (who served as prime minister from 1932 to 1946), Tage Erlander (prime minister from 1946 to 1969), and Olof Palme (who succeeded Erlander in October 1969). Experienced apprentices in day-to-day party affairs prior to their elevation as chairman, all four leaders eschewed ideological abstraction in favor of a realistic appreciation of the political feasibility of Socialist goals.

The Socialists' inclination toward collaboration with non-socialist political and economic forces was confirmed by their decision to join the Liberals in the coalition of 1917 and their restraint in implementing partisan policies after they assumed long-term executive leadership in 1932. Never abandoning their collectivist commitment to achieve positive conditions of individual equality and security, the Social Democrats have sought throughout their nearly 40 years in cabinet office to channel transforming change through established pluralist structures. Active government intervention in the economy to promote full employment, rather than extensive nationalization of industry, and comprehensive welfare services, rather than the forceful suppression of privileged socioeconomic strata, have thus been the principal features of Social Democratic radical reform efforts.[16]

[16] Richard Tomasson interprets these features of Socialist policies as a decline of ideology in "The Extraordinary Success of the Swedish Social Democrats," *The Journal of Politics*, 31 (August 1969), 772–798. That the Socialists remain ideologically receptive to some of the demands of the radical liberals and the New Left, however, is revealed in their recent policy initiatives discussed on pp. 139–140 and in Chapter Seven.

Table 10 Percentage of Popular Vote, 1914–1970

Year	Type of Election[a]	Electoral Participation	Conservatives	Center	Liberals
1914	N	66.2	36.5	0.2	26.9
1916	C	56.0	40.1	0.4	29.3
1917	N	65.8	24.7	8.5	27.6
1918	C	54.5	30.4	10.0	27.3
1919	C	63.3	24.9	13.2	25.4
1920	N	55.3	27.9	14.2	21.8
1921	N	54.2	25.8	11.1	19.1
1922	C	38.2	31.8	11.9	17.1
1924	N	53.0	26.1	10.8	16.9
1926	C	49.8	28.9	11.7	16.1
1928	N	67.4	29.4	11.2	15.9
1930	C	58.2	28.4	12.5	13.5
1932	N	68.6	23.5	14.1	11.7
1934	C	63.6	24.2	13.3	12.5
1936	N	74.5	17.6	14.3	12.9
1938	C	66.0	17.8	12.6	12.2
1940	N	70.3	18.0	12.0	12.0
1942	C	66.8	17.6	13.2	12.4
1944	N	71.9	15.9	13.6	12.9
1946	C	72.0	14.9	13.6	15.6
1948	N	82.7	12.3	12.4	22.8
1950	C	80.5	12.3	12.3	21.7
1952	N	79.1	14.4	10.7	24.4
1954	C	79.1	15.7	10.3	21.7
1956	N	79.8	17.1	9.4	23.8
1958	N[c]	77.4	19.5	12.7	18.2
1958	C	79.2	20.4	13.1	15.6
1960	N	85.9	16.5	13.6	17.5
1962	C	81.0	15.5	13.1	17.1
1964	N	83.9	13.7	13.2	17.0
1966	C	82.8	14.7	13.7	16.7
1968	N	89.3	12.9	15.7	14.3
1970	N	88.2	11.5	19.9	16.2

THE NONSOCIALIST BLOC

Despite persistent Socialist domination of the national executive for the past four decades, the three nonsocialist parties have maintained their status as representatives of nearly half of the Swedish electorate. When the Social Democrats assumed cabinet office in 1932, the Center, Liberal, and Moderate Unity parties together claimed 49.3 percent of the popular vote; their share of electoral support declined to 42 percent in 1940, but during the postwar period it has never fallen below 45.5 percent of the total. In two postwar elections (1956 and 1958) the nonsocialist parties have received, as a bloc, an absolute majority.

Year	Type of Election[a]	Electoral Participation	Cons.+ Cen.+ Libs.[b]	Cen.+ Libs.	SD	Com.	Other
1914	N	66.2			36.4		0.0
1916	C	56.0			30.2		0.0
1917	N	65.8			39.2		0.0
1918	C	54.5			32.3		0.0
1919	C	63.3			36.3		0.2
1920	N	55.3			36.1		0.0
1921	N	54.2			39.4	4.6	0.0
1922	C	38.2			34.7	4.5	0.0
1924	N	53.0			41.1	5.1	0.0
1926	C	49.8			39.0	4.1	0.2
1928	N	67.4			37.0	6.4	0.1
1930	C	58.2			37.0	6.4	0.1
1932	N	68.6			41.7	8.3	0.7
1934	C	63.6			42.1	6.8	1.1
1936	N	74.5			45.9	7.7	1.6
1938	C	66.0			50.4	5.7	1.3
1940	N	70.3			53.8	4.2	0.0
1942	C	66.8			50.3	5.9	0.6
1944	N	71.9			46.7	10.3	0.7
1946	C	72.0			44.4	11.2	0.3
1948	N	82.7			46.1	6.3	0.1
1950	C	80.5			48.6	4.9	0.2
1952	N	79.1			46.1	4.3	0.1
1954	C	79.1			47.4	4.8	0.1
1956	N	79.8			44.6	5.0	0.1
1958	N[c]	77.4			46.2	3.4	0.0
1958	C	79.2			46.8	4.0	0.1
1960	N	85.9			47.8	4.5	0.1
1962	C	81.0			50.5	3.8	0.0
1964	N	83.9	1.5	0.3	47.3	5.2	1.8
1966	C	82.8	2.6	1.7	42.2	6.4	1.9
1968	N	89.3	1.7	0.9	50.1	3.0	1.5
1970	N	88.2			45.3	4.8	2.2

[a]N stands for national elections; C stands for communal elections.
[b]Local electoral alliances.
[c]Special dissolution election.

Unlike the Social Democrats, the nonsocialist parties have failed to function as a cohesive aggregation of sociopolitical forces. Corresponding to what Dahl classifies as a policy-oriented nonstructural opposition,[17] the three bourgeois parties have differed significantly in ideological emphasis and their leaders' perceptions of political strategy and appropriate sites of opposition participation in the decision-making process.

[17] Dahl, pp. 332–347.

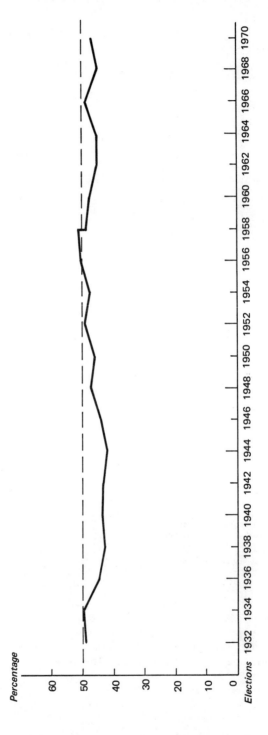

Figure 3 Aggregate Percentage of Nonsocialist Electoral
Support, 1932–1970

The Liberal Party

No other party encompasses as wide a diversity of interests in contemporary Sweden as the Liberals. Supported by civil servants, businessmen, workers, intellectuals, free thinkers, devout sectarians, and prohibitionists, the Liberal party presents a relatively united ideological front only on the basis of its vaguely defined espousal of social-liberal principles that differ from those of the Social Democrats more in nuance than in content.

Although the Liberals endorse the general aims of social welfare policies that have been implemented by the Socialists since the mid-1930s, they vigorously reject doctrinaire conceptions of how society should be organized. Nils Andrén has described the Liberal program as one seeking to realize "the social political goals of the Social Democrats in a society that gives increased freedom of movement to the individual citizens."[18]

Contemporary Swedish Liberals distinguish between limited government intervention in economic matters, which they view as necessary to insure full employment and a steady expansion of the national economy, and more encompassing measures to extend greater state control over investments and the direction of general economic development. The 1962 Liberal program proclaims:

> A more rapid increase in production demands greater capital resources. That society which creates the best prerequisites for the private ownership of property for all achieves in the long run the highest accumulation of capital and the most rapid progress. . . . Production should be regulated by those values of citizens that become evident in the economy of a society exemplifying freedom of choice. Human beings should not be forced to adjust their consumption according to production norms dictated by the state. Liberalism opposes any concentration of power, either by the state or by individuals, over access to capital and its utilization.[19]

Consistent with their programmatic principles, the Liberals recognize the necessity of increasing public expenditures to finance an extension of existing welfare services, but they oppose attempts to "socialize" the formulation of capital through taxation policies that might jeopardize personal and corporate savings. In addition

---

[18] Nils Andrén, *Svensk statskunskap* (Stockholm: Bokförlaget Liber, 1963), p. 47.

[19] Wieslander, p. 82.

the Liberals have pressed for greater fiscal economies on the part of the government and for minor tax reductions wherever they prove feasible.

Steeped in a tradition proclaiming the primacy of reason, equality, and freedom, which originated in the Age of Enlightenment and drew its early inspiration from the American and French revolutions, Swedish Liberalism enjoyed its zenith of popularity in the first decade and a half of the present century. As a unified political force the Liberal party dates from 1900, although several liberal factions had emerged within and outside the Riksdag during the latter part of the nineteenth century to advocate an extension of suffrage rights and the abolition of protective tariffs.

The Liberal party quickly succeeded in mobilizing extensive popular support for its demands to reform the Swedish electoral system, and by 1902 had become the largest party in the second chamber. In response to joint Liberal-Social Democratic agitation to broaden suffrage rights, the Conservatives introduced universal manhood suffrage and proportional representation in the reforms of 1907–1909. Under the leadership of Nils Edén, the Liberals subsequently joined the Social Democrats in the coalition ministry of 1917–1920 to introduce equal rights for women, abolish remaining suffrage restrictions in elections to the upper house, and complete the democratization of parliament by establishing the principle of cabinet government.

With the introduction of universal suffrage the Liberals fell victim to their own success. Having achieved their major demands with the passage of the second suffrage reform bill, the Liberals experienced a marked decline in electoral strength—losing support primarily to the Social Democrats. By 1921 their percentage of the national vote had dwindled from a high of 40.2 percent in 1911 to 19.1 percent.

A consultative referendum that was held in 1922 to determine public sentiment on prohibition resulted in a total rupture within Liberal ranks. The party split into a liberal urban faction (*Liberala partiet*) headed by Eliel Löfgren and a majority prohibitionist wing (*Frisinnade Folkpartiet*) under Carl Gustaf Ekman.

As no party yet claimed a stable majority in the Riksdag, the Prohibitionist Liberals, who at no time had more than 20 seats in the lower house, played a pivotal role during the era of minority parliamentarism (1920–1932).[20] Exploiting fully the strategic

[20] Rustow, *The Politics of Compromise*, pp. 91–101. See also Olle Nyman, *Parlamentarismen i Sverige* (Stockholm: Medborgarskolans Bokförlag, 1961), pp. 28–72.

central position of his group within parliament, Ekman alternately supported the Social Democrats and the Conservatives in pursuing Liberal policy goals to reduce proposed defense and welfare expenditures. The result was that during the first decade after the victory of parliamentary democracy in Sweden no cabinet could rule without tactical support from the Liberals. On two occasions the Liberals assumed direct ministerial responsibilities themselves: in 1926 Ekman formed a coalition with Löfgren's urban group, and from 1930 to 1932 the Prohibitionist Liberals governed alone.

The Liberals lost their status as a "balancer" between parties of the left and right when the Social Democrats came to power in 1932 and secured a promise of informal support from the Agrarians. Recognizing the weakness of continued disunity under such circumstances, leaders of the two liberal factions negotiated a merger in 1934 under the name People's party (*Folkpartiet*), the title that is used today.

Throughout the rest of the decade and during the early 1940s the united Liberal party retained approximately the same percentage of electoral support as the two liberal factions had held previously (that varied between 12.5 and 12.9 percent). Under the chairmanship of Gustaf Andersson i Rasjön, who became party leader in 1935, the Liberals concentrated their efforts during this period on building up internal cohesion without undertaking any major ideological innovations. In 1939 the Liberals joined the national wartime coalition government.

In the mid-1940s the Liberals adopted a program of "social liberalism" as the party's new doctrine. Its emphasis on social policies underscored Liberal acceptance of the welfare measures that had been promulgated by the Social Democrats after 1936. Concurrently the Liberals abandoned their earlier insistence on an unregulated market in favor of limited government intervention to insure full employment and sustained economic growth.

Liberal electoral strength rose to 12.9 percent in 1944, coinciding with Bertil Ohlin's appointment as party chairman, and by 1948 the Liberals had displaced the Conservatives as the largest nonsocialist party in the lower house. Ohlin's buoyant personality and skill as a seasoned debater undoubtedly contributed to the Liberal resurgence. Combining his academic training in economics with the practitioner's knowledge of political tactics that he had acquired as leader of the Liberal youth movement, Ohlin succeeded in projecting an image of intellectual versatility that greatly enhanced the party's stature. Except for a two-year interval

(1958–1960) the Liberals retained their position as the largest nonsocialist party in parliament throughout his tenure as chairman.

Ohlin's retirement in 1966 presaged a temporary decline in Liberal strength. He was initially succeeded by vice-chairman Sven Wedén, but after the party's loss of nine seats in the 1968 election Gunnar Helén—a former provincial governor—was elected the new Liberal chairman.

The Center Party

Once a narrowly based agrarian interest association, the Center party has in postwar years attempted to compensate for a continuing decline in the rural population by expanding its appeal to as wide a spectrum of potential voters as possible. In 1957 the Center adopted its present name and asserted its contemporary role as a "middle party" representing the interests of the urban middle-class as well as farmers.[21]

The Center adopted a new program in 1959 stressing the need to improve the economic status of small businessmen, strengthen the home environment through taxation and social policies favorable to families with children, and raise the general level of education. In addition, the Center seeks to counteract what the party views as potentially oppressive features of a greater concentration of power on the national level through "a policy that promotes local self-government, a decentralized construction of homes and industry, and a rich provincial and local cultural life."[22]

As a result of its refurbished political image and new program, the Center party has become relatively more heterogeneous than has been the case historically. Although agrarian elements continue to provide the major source of Center electoral strength, the party attracts the support of more than a quarter of Sweden's smaller businessmen and white-collar workers.

The personal leadership qualities of Gunnar Hedlund, who served as party chairman from 1949 to 1971, contributed to the Center's recent electoral advances. An astute politician exuding a down-to-earth charm, which he acquired from his agrarian forebears in northern Sweden, Hedlund exemplified many of the popu-

[21] The Center shares its self-designation as a middle party with the Liberals; the term is intended to indicate a programmatic position between Social Democrats and Conservatives.

[22] Wieslander, p. 39.

list elements that have exerted an important influence on Swedish history during the past century. He was succeeded in July 1971 by Thörnbjörn Fälldin, the Center's first vice-chairman, who also comes from an agrarian background in the northern provinces and has pursued simultaneous careers in the state administration and the party hierarchy.

The party was founded in 1913 in response to a call for agrarian unity led by Carl Berglund, a farmer-publisher in southwestern Sweden, after the disintegration of the Ruralist party. In 1915 a second ruralist organization, the Agrarian National Association (*Jordbrukarnas Riksförbund*), was formed in southern Sweden. The two groupings quickly attracted the allegiance of smaller landowners and farmers, many of whom had previously supported either the Conservatives or the Liberals, and in 1917 succeeded in winning a combined total of 14 seats in the lower house of the Riksdag. After increasing their representation to 30 deputies in the 1920 election, the parties merged in 1921 as the Agrarian party (*Bondeförbundet*). Agrarian electoral support dropped from 14.2 percent recorded in 1920 to 11.1 percent in the 1921 election (the first in which universal suffrage was applied) but remained relatively constant at the latter level throughout the rest of the decade.

During the 1920s the Agrarians emphasized cooperation with the Conservatives because of the latter's traditional affinity with ruralist interests and the joint opposition by both parties to increased state expenditures. Falling agricultural prices caused by the international economic crisis, however, resulted in a fundamental reorientation in the party's political stance. In the 1932 election the Agrarians increased their share of the national vote to 14.1 percent, while the number of Agrarian deputies in the second chamber rose to 36. Foresaking their earlier alignment with the right, the Agrarians entered into an informal alliance with the Social Democrats in early 1933 to endorse the government's antidepression program.

The Agrarians formed a three-month provisional minority cabinet with party chairman Axel Pehrsson-Bramstorp as prime minister in 1936, but joined a formal coalition with the Social Democrats after the fall election. With the outbreak of war in 1939, membership in the cabinet was broadened in response to Agrarian demands to include leaders of the Liberal and Conservative parties. The Agrarians entered a third coalition with the Socialists in 1951, but resigned six years later.

A principal reason for the Agrarians' dissociation from the

Social Democrats in 1957 was a steady decline in the party's electoral fortunes after 1951. Party support fell from 30 deputies in 1948 to 26 in the 1952 election, representing a decline in electoral strength from 12.4 percent to 10.7. Center support decreased even further in 1956 when the party's percentage of the popular vote reached a nadir of 9.4.

The party resigned from the government in 1957 after a national referendum, conducted to determine the electorate's preference among three alternative pension proposals, revealed that 15.0 percent of the voters favored the Agrarians' position. Campaigning under its new designation as the Center party, the party increased its strength from 19 to 32 seats in the dissolution election the following year. In seven subsequent elections Center elector support has averaged over 13 percent, reaching its highest level (19.9 percent) in 1970.

The Moderate Unity Party

Throughout modern Swedish history the Moderate Unity party, which was known until 1968 literally as the Right party, has continually had to redefine the meaning of conservatism in response to a continuing process of economic and sociopolitical transformation.[23] Historically collectivist in the tradition of Burkean and nineteenth-century continental (for example, Bismarckian) conservatism, Swedish Conservatives emerged in the twentieth century as the nation's most outspoken proponents of classical liberal economic and political individualism. In recent years the Conservatives have come to accept the basic principles of the modern welfare state, but continue to resist the centralizing consequences of Socialist radical reform policies in the name of individual autonomy and the sanctity of private ownership.

Nineteenth-century Conservative tenets advocating the retention of an oligarchical-paternalistic state were abandoned as a new generation of party leaders, representing the rising forces of economic and social modernization, emerged, who affirmed laissez faire capitalism and limited government authority. Conceding the inevitability of Liberal-Socialist reform efforts to democratize the political system, Sweden's Conservatives actively sponsored the suffrage reform of 1907–1909 and endorsed that of 1919–1921.

---

[23] See in particular Erik Anners, "Conservatism in Sweden," in M. Donald Hancock and Gideon Sjoberg (eds.), *Politics in the Post-Welfare State: Responses to the New Individualism* (New York: Columbia University Press, 1972).

During the 1920s and 1930s the Conservatives resisted the Social Democrats' proposed social reform measures on the grounds of excessive costs and high taxes, but the demonstrated success and popularity of welfare services induced party leaders by the mid-1940s to modify their attitudes toward social reform policies. Successive Conservative programs of 1946 and 1956 affirmed the need for collective social security provisions to improve general living conditions, but stressed as a matter of ideological principle that "private enterprise and individual property rights are the best means [to guarantee] economic development."[24]

Persisting characteristics of the Moderate Unity party, therefore, have been an emphasis on the preservation of existing structures and an adjustment of its ideology in reactive response to prior changes in the domestic environment. With the adoption of a new "humanistic conservative" program in December 1969, the renamed Moderate Unity party has assumed a more positive attitude toward sociopolitical transformation. Reiterating its defense of private ownership and a competitive economic system, the Moderate Unity party nonetheless calls for concerted social action to deal with issues of common concern such as the preservation of ecological balance. The new program asserts that "a good environment should, in principle, be considered a socioeconomic resource, and its costs should be calculated with reference to the common values we wish to protect and strengthen."[25]

Politically, the Moderate Unity party views the Swedish state as "the common service organization of the citizens, . . ."[26] and defines the goal of social security as enabling "all persons, to the greatest possible extent, to live well both physically and psychologically under socially equitable conditions."[27] To help mitigate the effects of increasing bureaucratization of public and private organizations, the party advocates the decentralization of decision-making authority—for example, in higher education and the labor market—to maximize individual responsibility and participation.[28]

The lineal ancestor of the Moderate Unity party is the Rural-

[24] Wieslander, p. 39.

[25] Moderata samlingsparti, *Program* (Stockholm: Moderata samlingspartiet, 1969). (Mimeographed.) The program was adopted at an extraordinary party congress on November 21–23, 1969. Hereafter referred to as *Program*.

[26] *Program*, p. 29.

[27] *Program*, p. 12.

[28] *Program*, pp. 21 and 23.

ist party (*Lantmannapartiet*), founded in the lower house in 1867. Throughout the latter part of the nineteenth century Conservative spokesmen in the Riksdag represented the interests of farmers, larger landowners, and higher administrative bureaucrats. But with the advance of industrialization since the 1890s the Conservatives have become primarily an urban-based party, drawing most of their electoral support from industrialists, employers, and high-level white-collar workers.

The introduction of manhood and later universal suffrage resulted in both a reduction and consolidation of Conservative strength. Faced with a steady decline in parliamentary representation due to sustained electoral gains registered by the Liberals and the Social Democrats, Conservative deputies assembled forces in 1912 to found a National party (*Nationella partiet*) in the upper house and a Rural and Citizens' party (*Lantmanna och borgarepartiet*) in the lower chamber. Arvid Lindman, an industrialist, became chairman of the lower house faction the same year, thereby establishing himself as the dominant figure in modern Swedish Conservatism despite his personal rivalry with Ernst Trygger, chairman of the Senate group. The Conservatives assumed ministerial power twice during the interwar period, first under Trygger (1923–1924) and later under Lindman (1928–1930).

Following Trygger's resignation as chairman of the upper house faction in 1935, the two parliamentary groups merged to form a united Conservative party (*Riksdagshögern*).[29] Gösta Bagge, formerly a professor of economics and founder of the Conservative periodical, *Svensk tidskrift* (*Swedish Journal*), was appointed leader that same year. He served in that capacity until 1944 when Fritiof Domö, a farmer, was designated chairman.

Conservative strength fell steadily after the Social Democrats assumed cabinet responsibility in 1932, primarily as a result of the party's continued resistance to the government's social welfare measures. By 1948 the Conservatives not only lost their previous status as Sweden's largest nonsocialist party but were reduced to the position of the smallest.

The Conservative defeat led to a change in party leadership two years later, establishing a pattern that the Conservatives have followed after most subsequent electoral setbacks, when Jarl H. Hjalmarsson was elected chairman. A lawyer with close ties among Sweden's leading industrialists, Hjalmarsson sought to

---

[29] The party's national organization adopted the name of *Högerns riksorganisation* in 1938. The party officially designated itself as *Högerpartiet* (The   ᵃʳᵗᵛ) in 1952. Andrén, *Svensk statskunskap*, p. 41.

steer a middle course between tacit acceptance of social welfare principles and sustained opposition to a further extension of state services that would mean increased taxes. Throughout the 1950s this strategy seemed to succeed. In 1952 the Conservatives became the second largest nonsocialist party in the lower house, and from 1958 to 1960 dominated opposition ranks with 45 seats, compared to 38 for the Liberals and 32 for the Center.

After a major Conservative loss in the 1960 general election, because of, in large measure, the party's demand for extensive tax reductions that would have meant a restriction of welfare services, Hjalmarsson resigned in 1961 to become director of the Swedish Employers' Confederation. Gunnar Heckscher was appointed party chairman in his place.

Heckscher, a professor of political science at the University of Stockholm, injected a new element of flexibility into the style of Conservative policies. Having served as chairman of the party's youth movement from 1945 to 1952, Heckscher possessed impressive credentials as a skilled orator and intellectual. He deliberately strove to create a positive image of a Conservative party intent on endorsing comprehensive welfare measures and cooperating with the Liberals and Center in an effort to form a united nonsocialist ideological front, but floundered in his attempts to preserve factional unity among younger progressives and older recalcitrants. Confronted with a party revolt in southern Sweden in favor of a unified nonsocialist electoral alliance in 1964 and charged by many of his party lieutenants with a major share of responsibility for the subsequent Conservative loss of seven seats in the September election,[30] Heckscher announced his resignation in March 1965. Yngve Holmberg, a 40-year-old businessman and Conservative party secretary, became chairman the following June.

Under Holmberg's leadership a program committee was appointed in 1964, whose recommendations for revision led to the adoption of the party program in 1969, and the party's name was changed to that of Moderate Unity party. In the 1966 communal election the Conservatives increased their percentage of the popular vote to 14.7, but their support declined in the following two elections to parliament. One result was that the party congress voted in the fall of 1970 to replace Holmberg with Gösta Bohman, formerly vice-chairman and a member of parliament since 1958.

[30] The formation of the electoral alliance in Malmö is discussed on pp. 134–135.

THE LEFT PARTY-COMMUNISTS

As the smallest force in Sweden's tripartite party system, the Left Party-Communists have never been able to entertain long-term hopes of acquiring direct ministerial responsibility. Instead, Communist leaders have concentrated—much in the same manner as third parties in the United States—on acquiring an indirect influence on government policies.

Something of an anomaly in the annals of the International Communist movement, the Left Party-Communists in Sweden embody a tradition of revisionism engendered by a combination of cultural, historical, and political factors. Although they remain ideologically faithful to the theoretical principles of Marxism-Leninism, the Swedish Communists have been inhibited by forces of restraint inherent in Sweden's political culture that similarly induced the Social Democrats to pursue a course of moderation. Thus they have hesitated to promote rigid policies in an obstinate manner.

Moreover, the Swedish Communists have traditionally pursued a "national" policy that has facilitated tactical flexibility in response to distinctive Swedish conditions. This tendency is rooted in the party's financial independence of the Soviet-dominated Third International during the formative years of the Communist movement in Sweden.[31] After the end of World War II, despite the vicissitudes of the cold war, the leaders of the Communist party continued to stress their national independence, supporting the Soviet bloc in foreign policy declarations but domestically promoting a popular front policy.[32]

A final factor encouraging Communist inclination toward moderation has been the tenuous political balance within parliament during the postwar period. On several occasions the Communists have supplied the Social Democrats with tactical support in crucial joint votes in which the government party lacked a majority in its own right. For example, Communist abstention saved a Socialist proposal to implement a general sales tax from certain defeat in 1959. Initially the Communists had joined the nonsocialist parties in opposing the measure, but when a joint vote was called they abstained to prevent a government crisis.[33] A

[31] Franz Borkenau, *The Communist International* (London: Faber and Faber, Ltd., 1938), p. 347. Also see Sven Rydenfelt, *Kommunismen i Sverige* (Lund: Gleerupska Universitätsbokhandeln, 1954).

[32] For their part the Social Democrats have steadfastly refused Communist proffers of electoral or political cooperation.

[33] Nyman, *Parlamentarismen i Sverige*, p. 115.

former party secretary justified this policy on the grounds that Communist opposition to the Social Democrats would mean a victory for the nonsocialist parties. "The bourgeois parties have abused the government because they want to take over control themselves," he said. "We have voted with the Social Democrats so the government could be saved."[34]

In affluent, welfare-oriented Sweden the fate of the Communist party seemed throughout the early postwar period to confirm Seymour Lipset's thesis that there is a direct relation between increased economic development and a decline (or absence) of left-wing radicalism.[35] Drawing principally on industrial employees in urban areas and timber and mining workers in the northern provinces for the core of their electoral support, the Communists had attracted an average following of only 5 percent from the early twenties onward. Their percentage of the popular vote reached a zenith of 11.2 in 1945, thanks principally to the temporary prestige of the Soviet Union as one of the victorious wartime allies, but by 1958 the percentage had plummeted to 3.4.

Beginning in the early 1960s the rise of an internal New Left opposition resulted in a fundamental change in the party's ideological characteristics. After Hermanssons' election as party chairman in 1964, the Swedish Communists began to move in the direction of left radicalism chartered since the beginning of the decade by the Socialist People's parties in Denmark and Norway. Like their ideological counterparts in the neighboring Scandinavian systems, the Communists emphasized their autonomy from Moscow and simultaneously sought to project an image of ideological purity untainted by the compromises with pluralist and economic forces that the Social Democrats have made as responsible office holders.

The specific demands of the revitalized New Left-Communist movement were spelled out in a new program that was adopted at the party's twenty-second congress in May 1967. The party's vision of a "Socialist alternative" to established Swedish society, based on the classical Marxist refutation of capitalism, includes demands for industrial democracy; increased power of consumers to control "the direction of production, its quality and prices; . . ." an expanded public economic sector; the transfer of banks, private insurance companies, and key industries to public ownership; and

---

[34] Private interview.
[35] S. M. Lipset, *Political Man* (New York: Anchor Books, 1963), pp. 31 and 45–58.

the structural reform of public administration to create a state "that is open and responsible to the people, defends their interests, and realizes their will."[36]

Characteristic New Left elements in the program, which distinguish it from earlier Communist ideological tenets, are the party's prescriptions for the socialization of the economy and its view of civil liberties. First, the Left Party-Communists do not view nationalization, in the traditional sense of direct state ownership of the means of production, as a panacea for the ostensible shortcomings of capitalist society. Instead the program calls for a decentralized model of socialism in which public ownership of major companies and credit institutions would be dispersed among "the state, provincial assemblies, local communes, and producer and consumer cooperatives."[37] Second, the Left Party-Communists explicitly affirm "the free formation of opinion, universal and equal suffrage, parliamentarism, and decisions according to the majority principle."[38] Even under the projected attainment of Left Party-Communist goals in a classless socialist society, such liberties would remain in force. As the new program proclaims:

> Socialism is not a static condition devoid of conflict. . . . Differences will remain between people and groups, between ideas and interests. They would no longer be hindered or distorted, however, by the power relations prevailing in the former class society. Instead, they can be freely discussed and rationally solved. The free exchange of opinion would become the conscious driving force in social development.[39]

Conceding that the Social Democrats have helped implement significant gains on behalf of working-class interests such as political democracy, a higher standard of living, and social security, the Left Party-Communists criticize the majority party for failing to achieve basic changes in power and economic relations. "The Social Democrats have administered the capitalist society," the new program asserts. "The conscious socialist forces have not been strong enough to dismantle class society."[40] Therefore the Left Party-Communists, as a "part of the working-class movement," view as their self-appointed task an initiating role in inten-

---

36 Vänsterpartiet-kommunisterna, *Samling vänster i svensk politik* (Göteborg: Västan tryckeri AB, 1967), p. 37. Hereafter referred to as *Samling Vänster*.

37 *Samling Vänster*, p. 37.

38 *Samling Vänster*, p. 29.

39 *Samling Vänster*, p. 38.

40 *Samling Vänster*, p. 33.

sifying "political activity and cooperation" with "all left social forces" in Swedish society to promote the conscious pursuit of socialist democracy.[41]

Because of their new ideological and tactical flexibility, the Left Party-Communists succeeded in reversing their earlier electoral decline by gaining three seats at the expense of the Social Democrats in 1964. They continued their advance in the 1966 election, but suffered a major setback, as a result of the Soviet occupation of Czechoslovakia in 1968.

THE DIALECTICS OF PARTY CHANGE

Change in Sweden's party characteristics has occurred through a process of dialectical tension among the three major components of the multiparty system. As the majority party in parliament, the Social Democrats have utilized their control of cabinet office to initiate successive steps of gradualist system transformation, seeking throughout the postwar period to maximize economic security and productivity and to extend the scope of welfare services under the banner of social solidarity. The success as well as the alleged inadequacies of Socialist policies have consequently stimulated both a partial consolidation of the nonsocialist bloc and the internal transfiguration of the Left Party-Communists. Simultaneous nonsocialist and New Left attacks on government policies prompted countersocialist initiatives in the form of a new program of socioeconomic transformation.

During the first three decades after the Social Democrats assumed executive leadership, a relatively stable pattern of "competitive-bargaining" relations prevailed among the nonsocialist parties and between them and the Social Democrats.[42] Strictly competitive in elections, nonsocialist leaders concentrated on enhancing their capacity to influence government policies principally by maintaining or increasing their relative share of popular support. Between elections the Center party bargained directly with the Socialists as junior partners in two coalitions, while the Liberals and Conservatives pursued more diffuse bargaining tactics aimed at modifying policy decisions during deliberations in parliamentary committees and on Royal Commissions. The Commu-

[41] *Samling Vänster*, pp. 29 and 35.

[42] The terminology, "competitive-bargaining relations," is derived from Dahl, pp. 336–338.

nists were similarly competitive in elections, but tacitly supported the Social Democratic cabinet in parliament despite sustained Socialist rebuffs to their proffers of policy collaboration.

Established relations within the party system began to change when the Social Democrats introduced legislation to create a program of supplementary pension benefits in 1957.[43] By resigning from the cabinet and joining the Liberals and Conservatives in common opposition to the Socialist proposal, the Center party contributed the immediate impetus for a gradual convergence of nonsocialist forces. As a result party competition increasingly assumed Socialist-nonsocialist dimensions, paralleling simultaneous processes of party system realignment in Norway and Denmark.

Conflict and Unity

In broader perspective the Center's decision to withdraw from the government reflected an emerging consensus that the nonsocialist parties shared common interests in resisting Socialist domination of the national executive. Confronting the cabinet's determination to press for a partisan (Socialist) solution to the pension issue, nonsocialist leaders perceived that the balance of Sweden's postwar political equilibrium was on the verge of tipping decisively in favor of the Social Democrats. This view seemed confirmed when the Socialists revealed that they preferred to remain in office as a minority cabinet rather than form a national four-party coalition as nonsocialist spokesmen had previously urged. Hence the three opposition leaders began to stress interparty policy coordination as the necessary basis for a possible alternative government.

Reinforcing the evolution of nonsocialist cohesion in reaction to entrenched Socialist cabinet rule was the confluence of nonsocialist ideology during the postwar period. By the late 1950s widespread popular acceptance of the welfare state had significantly mitigated the ideological cleavages that had once separated the nonsocialist parties. Despite the origin of the Center party as an agrarian interest association and the historical antagonisms between the Liberals and the Conservatives, the three parties had come to share broadly similar concepts of how society and the economy should be organized.

Underlying the coalescence of nonsocialist ideology was demographic and social change. As urbanization and economic diversification generated a continued expansion of white-collar workers,

---

[43] The supplementary pension debate is discussed in Chapter Eight.

traditional socioeconomic sources of electoral support no longer sufficed as a guarantee that the nonsocialist parties could maintain their relative share of popular support. "To the extent that all major parties are permeated by the opinion and attitudes of these groups," Otto Kirchheimer has observed, "one may justifiably say that diminished social polarization and diminished political polarization are going hand in hand."[44] Forced to compete with the Social Democrats and each other for the same marginal voters among salaried employees, Sweden's nonsocialist leaders concluded that a tactical requisite for challenging Socialist hegemony was to harmonize their policies rather than dissipate energies in self-defeating strife.

The emergence of the radical liberals contributed an additional impetus to greater nonsocialist bloc unity. By emphasizing the need to formulate a common program of sociopolitical transformation based on "progressive, social, and liberal tenets,"[45] leaders of the Liberal and Center youth associations helped prompt an internal debate within both of the middle parties on principles of a positive alternative to the policies of the Social Democrats. Their proposals for party and social reform, while restricted to the Liberals and the Center, found an appreciable echo among some Conservatives as well, in particular within the Conservative Youth Association and in local branches of the Conservative party in southern Sweden.

The specific forms that nonsocialist coalescence might assume have been the object of continuing controversy within opposition ranks. Initially Center spokesmen, after their withdrawal from the cabinet in 1957, aligned themselves with the Conservatives in a more outspoken critique of the Socialist pension proposal than the position adopted by the Liberals. But once the conflict was settled on Socialist terms in 1959, the Center abandoned its informal alliance with the Conservatives and by 1960 joined the Liberals in endorsing the new program of compulsory supplementary pensions, thereby paving the way for intensified cooperation between the two middle parties. During the remainder of the decade opposition leaders pursued two, at times conflicting, strategies in their attempt to intensify bloc cohesion.

The first of these was directed toward enhancing nonsocialist bargaining leverage within parliament. Since the capacity of the

---

[44] Otto Kirchheimer, "The Waning of the Opposition in Parliamentary Regimes," *Social Research*, 24 (Summer 1957), 148.

[45] Per Ahlmark, *et al.*, *Mitt i 60-talet* (Stockholm: Bonniers, 1966), p. 88.

nonsocialist parties to influence executive policies derives in part from their parliamentary strength, opposition leaders placed high priority on presenting a common front in the Riksdag. Concerted nonsocialist efforts to coordinate parliamentary tactics date from January 1962 when Ohlin, chairman of the Liberal party, invited Center chairman Hedlund and Conservative leader Heckscher to consult jointly on the preparation of opposition motions and the coordination of committee strategies. In ensuing years, the Liberal initiative yielded an appreciable increase in nonsocialist cooperation on several policy levels. Informal consultations were instituted among opposition leaders to discuss general issues pending in the Riksdag and Royal Commissions; members of the three party secretariats intensified contacts before and during each parliamentary session in an attempt to coordinate nonsocialist motions; and the parties undertook increased policy coordination during committee deliberations.[46]

Because elections remain the decisive site of nonsocialist encounters with the Social Democrats, opposition spokesmen simultaneously attempted to maximize their aggregate electoral competitiveness. By the mid-1960s nonsocialist leaders were fully aware that if they were to present a credible alternative to the Socialist government they would have to overcome the historical image of bloc disunity. In contrast to their relative success in coordinating policies in parliament, however, they failed to achieve agreement on a positive electoral strategy for the nonsocialist bloc as a whole.

Following the 1962 communal election, in which all three opposition parties had suffered losses, Heckscher urged the Liberal and Center parties to join the Conservatives in forming a single electoral front prior to the 1964 election. Locally the proposal was put to a vote in February 1964 at a series of special party meetings in the "four-city constituency" in southern Sweden (which includes Malmö and three other cities in Malmöhus province). When a majority of Center delegates refused to endorse the Conservative initiative, the editors of two Conservative newspapers in Malmö, the *Sydsvenska Dagbladet* and *Kvällsposten*, instigated a revolt against the district party organizations. The renegades, who included Riksdag deputies from all three nonsocialist parties, organized the Citizens Rally (*Medborgerlig samling*) electoral alliance in an effort to present a common "pro-

46 Interview with former Liberal chairman, Bertil Ohlin. Nonsocialist parliamentary cooperation is discussed in Chapter Seven.

gressive" alternative to the Social Democrats. Unwilling to join the rebels, constituency leaders of the rump Liberal, Center, and Conservative parties decided to submit separate lists of candidates in the September election under the old party names.

On the national level, Ohlin and Hedlund affirmed their support of nonsocialist cooperation in principle, but rejected Heckscher's suggestion for a three-party electoral alliance on the grounds that the Conservatives still sought to state the nonsocialist cause in excessively negative terms. Rather than follow the Conservatives' lead in advocating policies clearly differentiated from those of the Social Democrats (such as Conservative efforts in 1962 to reduce taxes at the expense of child allowances), the chairmen of the Liberal and Center parties maintained that a nonsocialist program must be positive in tone and content.

The Liberal-Center strategy was predicated on the assumption that marginal voters could be won over to the nonsocialist bloc only through a policy of moderation. According to recent Swedish opinion surveys, nearly a third of the Liberal supporters and over a quarter of the Center followers would endorse the Social Democrats as their second party choice in contrast to 26.6 percent and 8.3 percent, respectively, who would prefer the Conservatives.[47] In case of cross pressures on marginal voters induced by a radicalization of nonsocialist policy goals to agree with the prevailing Conservative stance, the Liberals and Center could anticipate significant losses to the Socialists.

The potential public appeal of a unified progressive program seemed to be confirmed by the outcome of the 1964 election. In the four-city constituency the Citizens Rally amassed 27.8 percent of the district vote (compared to a combined total of 15.7 percent for the separate nonsocialist party lists) to win three seats in the Riksdag. On Gotland, where the Liberals and Center conducted a joint campaign, the two middle parties received 46.1 percent of the vote (compared to 39.5 percent for the Social Democrats and 14.4 for the Conservatives). Nationally, both the Liberals and the Center increased their share of popular electoral support, while conservative strength fell over three percentage points relative to the 1960 general election.

In light of their assessment of political preferences among marginal voters, Ohlin and Hedlund resolved that formal nonsocialist electoral cooperation must be limited to the Liberals and

---

[47] Survey data processed for the author by the Swedish Institute of Public Opinion Research (SIFO) in 1966.

the Center. Accordingly, the Liberal and Center chairman appointed in June 1965 a joint committee, made up of ten representatives from each party, to draw up a common campaign program for both parties prior to the 1966 communal election.

As members of the Liberal-Center "cooperation delegation" began consultations to draft the common program, events outside of Sweden tentatively resolved the tactical impasse on electoral strategy between the two middle parties and the Conservatives. In Norway the nonsocialist parties united on a common "Coalition Parties" program to defeat the incumbent Labor party in the September 1965 election to the Storting and formed the first stable alternative cabinet since 1935. Emulating the Norwegian example, the three opposition parties in Sweden declared a moratorium (*Borgfreden*) on intrabloc strife during the 1965–1966 winter session of Riksdag. This negative form of nonsocialist electoral unity was conceived of as an important test of future nonsocialist electoral prospects. Despite persisting differences between the Liberal-Center parties and the Conservatives, the three opposition leaders hoped that the outward display of harmony would enhance their aggregate bloc competitiveness with the Social Democrats and thereby enable the nonsocialist parties ultimately to gain a parliamentary majority. Coordinating policy goals could then await the formation of a nonsocialist cabinet.

The 1966 election provided an important test of electoral reaction to differing models of nonsocialist cooperation. With opposition leaders tacitly pledging to refrain from unnecessary attacks on each other during the campaign, the Liberals and Center formalized middle party electoral unity with the publication of their joint program—entitled Middle Cooperation (*Mittensamverkan*)—in June 1966. Party spokesmen viewed the program as a statement of "common goals to implement socially progressive policies on the basis of individual responsibility, a market economy, and free enterprise." Specifically, the two parties announced their determination "to hinder a Socialist . . . concentration of power" by pressing for the creation of a unicameral parliament, urged restraint in future state expenditures to reduce inflationary pressures on the economy, advocated better planning and the localization of industry outside the major urban areas as means to ease Sweden's housing shortage, and proposed appropriate tax adjustments and provisions for easier credit to farmers to stimulate more effective agricultural production.[48] Hedlund openly re-

[48] Folkpartiets and centerpartiets samarbetsdelegation, *Mittensamverkan* (Stockholm: Linkoln Bloms Boktryckeri, AB, 1966), p. 1.

ferred to the program as "an alternative to the policies of the Socialist government,"[49] while Ohlin emphasized the psychological importance of a concerted display of unity between the Liberal and Center parties as an inducement for the Conservatives to abandon their "extreme policies" of the past. A precondition for an eventual change of government in Sweden, Ohlin stated, is "for cooperation [among the nonsocialist parties] to be extended step by step in support of a reform oriented, truly competitive program."[50]

Efforts to translate the general *Borgfreden* among the three opposition parties and the concrete aspirations spelled out in the Liberal-Center program into an actual display of nonsocialist unity assumed a variety of forms. Local branches of the Liberal and Center parties combined forces in five constituencies (Stockholm, Lund, Gotland, Västernorrland, and Norrbotten) in support of a single list of candidates. In Landskrona, Ängelholm, and Mölndal, where local Conservative leaders proved willing to endorse the Liberal-Center principles, all three parties coalesced in a common electoral front. Leaders of the Citizens Rally once again submitted a united nonsocialist list in Malmö, while a minority of Liberal and Center delegates sponsored a separate Middle party slate. Candidates to the city council in Göteborg competed on a unified nonsocialist program but under separate party labels. Liberal and Conservatives formed an alliance in Hälsingborg, while the Conservatives and the Center joined forces in Västervik.

The New Left Challenge

To the left of the Social Democrats, the Communist party, equally desirous of change in government policies but of a vastly different sort, provided the second major impulse for change in Sweden's party system. Lars Herlitz, an alternate member of the party's executive committee, established the tone of Communist electoral strategy in a television debate early in the 1966 campaign, when he observed: "In recent years a radical and self-conscious opinion has arisen in our country calling for renewal in politics. But there exists a wide gulf between the demands of this opinion and the policies that are pursued."[51] To bridge the gap between the "res-

---

[49] Press conference on June 3, 1966. Quoted in *Dagens Nyheter*, June 4, 1966, p. 6.

[50] *Dagens Nyheter*, May 14, 1966, p. 4.

[51] Sveriges Radio, *Inför valet: Vad betyder din röst? Snabbprotokoll*, UM (August 22, 1966), p. 22.

toration of clear Socialist goals as the policy aim of the entire working-class movement" and Social Democratic "defense of the status quo," Communist chairman Hermansson viewed a Communist electoral advance as a potential lever to induce a radicalization of the majority party.[52] Refuting Social Democratic charges that the Communist strategy would weaken the Swedish left by dividing it,[53] Hermansson said: "We do not seek to split the working-class movement but are working toward gaining a greater share of influence."[54]

Explicitly appealing to New Left sentiment among Social Democrats and political radicals, the Communist chairman asserted that "many members in the Social Democratic party have the same opinion as the Communists concerning the necessity of engaging in a determined struggle to break the power of capital finance and build a Socialist society in Sweden . . . Those who want a development to the left can best express this demand by supporting the Communist party in the election. A communist gain will mean more steps to the left in Swedish politics."[55]

The combined attacks of the loosely united nonsocialist bloc and the reinvigorated Communist movement against government economic, welfare, and housing policies resulted in a defeat for the Social Democrats. Socialist strength fell from 47.3 percent (1964) to 42.4—its lowest point since 1934—which meant a loss of 146 seats in the local provincial and municipal assemblies. The nonsocialist parties won absolute majorities in Stockholm and Göteborg, thereby ending nearly a decade of Socialist dominance in each city, and 13 out of Sweden's 25 provincial assemblies. Their combined number of local assembly mandates increased from 784 to 884, with the various electoral alliances among two or more of the parties accounting for 95 of the 100 new seats. Nationally, total nonsocialist electoral strength rose from 44.2 percent (1964) to 49.6. The Communists registered advances uniformly throughout the nation and more than doubled their previous allotment of assembly seats, increasing their representation in the various regional and municipal assemblies from 30 to 79.

[52] Sveriges kommunistiska parti, *Tal vid SKP:s rikskonferense den 20 maj 1966* (Stockholm: Sveriges kommunistiska parti, 1966), p. 1. (Mimeographed.) Hereafter referred to as *Tal vid SKP:s rikskonferens.*

[53] Editorial in *Aftonbladet,* August 26, 1966, p. 2.

[54] Private interview.

[55] *Tal vid SKP:s rikskonferens,* pp. 14–15.

The Socialist Response

In response to the 1966 defeat the Social Democrats initiated a comprehensive series of policy innovations designed to meet many specific criticisms of their nonsocialist and Communist opponents. In rapid succession the Socialists reached agreement with the nonsocialist parties on the pending issue of constitutional reform, expanded the rate of new housing construction, and increased government efforts to encourage the localization of industry. Sensitive to New Left-inspired charges of government passivity in the face of persisting contradictions in modern pluralist-welfare society, the Socialists also undertook new government and party measures to extend the scope of collective responsibility for economic growth and individual security. In early 1967 they sponsored the creation of an Investment Corporation and a state Investment Bank, both of which are intended to stimulate industrial expansion and provide sources of credit in areas where private interests are unable or unwilling to invest, and they also convened an extraordinary party congress in October 1967 to consider the adoption of a new economic program.

The economic program, which was formally ratified at the party's twenty-third congress in June 1968,[56] constitutes the most ambitious attempt by the Social Democrats to define in concrete terms their conceptions of long-term socioeconomic goals. A product of joint collaboration between the Social Democrats and the LO, the new program notes that full employment and social security will not automatically result from ongoing processes of economic change. To insure that "individual security and justice" can be reconciled with "economic progress,"[57] the Social Democrats therefore advocated a significant extension of social influence over productive resources and economic planning. Such objectives would be promoted through an expansion of public corporations, the use of collective savings for investment in new industries, the direct participation by the state (for example, through the Development Corporation and the Investment Bank) in technological and economic development, the implementation of industrial democracy in individual enterprises, and a more active role by the government in determining and enforcing national economic guidelines.[58]

[56] Sveriges socialdemokratiska arbetareparti, *Program för aktiv näringspolitik. Näringspolitiska kommitténs slutrapport* (Stockholm: Sveriges socialdemokratiska arbetareparti, 1968). (Mimeographed.) Hereafter referred to as *Aktiv näringspolitik.*

[57] *Aktiv näringspolitik*, p. 3.

[58] *Aktiv näringspolitik*, pp. 4–10.

Although the flurry of government initiatives and the new economic program fell far short of the radical vision of structural transformation envisioned by Sweden's New Left, the Socialist response served to enhance the party's image among many potential dissidents as an activist force of socioeconomic change. Equally significant, announced Social Democratic intentions did not pose a direct challenge to either the principle of private ownership or pluralist processes of government, as their 27-point socialization program had appeared to do two decades earlier.[59] Indeed, as New Left spokesman Göran Therborn sarcastically observed, the Socialist economic program would actually lead to even closer cooperation between the Social Democrats and business interests, to the mutual advantage (in terms of economic stability) of both the marjority representatives of organized labor and private enterprise.[60]

Having adopted new policy measures that placated at least some of the nation's political radicals, while simultaneously refraining from drastic socialization steps that might alienate crucial middle-class strata, the Social Democrats confronted the 1968 parliamentary election with a number of solid accomplishments in office. Prime Minister Erlander stated the government party's case for a renewed electoral mandate when he declared at the Socialist congress in June: "Labor market and localization policies have been extended with expenditures of 520 million crowns. A security system for older unemployed persons has been introduced. The foreign assitance program has . . . been increased by 100 million crowns a year. . . . General pensions have been raised 450 million crowns. . . . New starts in housing construction have increased to 100,000 units. . . . This entire reform program . . . has been implemented with virtually no increase in taxes."[61]

Among nonsocialist forces the *Borgfreden* on overt intrabloc strife remained in force, and the Liberal-Center parties issued a revised Middle Cooperation program to underscore their continued commitment to a common opposition alternative.[62] Otherwise, no concerted effort had been made to coordinate the policies of all three parties in the form of a shadow cabinet program. Hedlund attempted to explain the absence of a positive strategy

[59] See Chapter Eight.

[60] *Dagens Nyheter*, October 18, 1967, p. 8.

[61] Sveriges socialdemokratiska arbetareparti, *Dagsprotokoll, Sveriges Socialdemokratiska Arbetarepartis 23:e kongress 9–15 juni 1968* (Stockholm: Tiden, 1968), p. 8.

[62] *Mittensamverkan 68* (Stockholm: Bokförlaget Folk & Samhälle, 1968).

among the three parties and what the electorate might expect of a nonsocialist victory, when he declared: "We have a detailed middle program as the basis for a new government. Cooperation with the Conservatives can be arranged without difficulty later, but we can't risk asking the Conservatives to cooperate before the election because the election would turn out badly. There is no common program. The program that doesn't exist will provide the basis for a coalition government. (*sic*)"[63]

Locally, nonsocialist electoral cooperation was formalized in two constituencies between the Liberals and the Center and among like-minded progressives who campaigned jointly under a "Unity 68" label (a successor to the Citizens Rally electoral alliance) in Malmö.

The Left Party-Communists entered the campaign with some of their ideological appeal diminished by the recent activism of the Social Democrats but still hopeful of an electoral advance. Public opinion surveys conducted in July had indicated that the party would receive 6.6 percent of the vote,[64] a small but symbolically important increase over its share of popular support in 1966. But on August 21 an international event occurred that proved a critical significance for Left Party-Communist prospects: the Soviet Union occupied Czechoslovakia, thereby reversing liberalizing tendencies under the Dubcek regime that had provided crucial indirect support for revisionist efforts in Sweden to redefine orthodox Marxist tenets. Although Hermansson promptly condemned the action and called for a suspension of Swedish diplomatic relations with the Soviet Union,[65] his party had already suffered irreparable damage in the eyes of marginal New Left voters. Given the ideological affinity between the theoretical underpinnings of the Soviet system and the socialist doctrines of the Left Party-Communists, Soviet policies in Czechoslovakia inevitably reflected adversely on the political reliability of the Swedish party.

The apparent success of Socialist policy initiatives, continued disunity between the Liberal-Center and Conservative parties, and the Soviet move into Czechoslovakia produced an impressive victory for the Social Democrats. Mobilizing many members of the LO who had abstained in the 1966 election as well as a sizable percentage of first-time voters, the Socialists received an absolute

---

[63] *Dagens Nyheter*, August 20, 1968, p. 10. Prime Minister Erlander replied: "Personally I believe you're going to too much trouble with a government program. You'll never need to have one."

[64] *Dagens Nyheter*, July 12, 1968, p. 12.

[65] Stockholm newspapers, August 23, 1968.

majority of 50.1 percent and increased their parliamentary representation from 113 seats to 125. Over 12,000 more persons voted for the nonsocialist bloc than in 1966, but the relative percentage of opposition strength fell to 45.5 percent. The total number of nonsocialist deputies in the lower house declined from 112 to 105. Within the nonsocialist bloc only the Center party managed to advance in strength, increasing its electoral percentage to 15.7 for a gain of four seats. The Liberals lost nine seats, and the Conservatives lost one. For the Left Party-Communists the election was an unmitigated disaster. The party lost five mandates—over half of its previous allotment of seats—and declined in electoral strength to the lowest point in the party's history (3 percent).

Having restored their electoral mandate, the Social Democrats proceeded to transfer leadership to the party's fourth generation. Erlander stepped down in October 1969 as Socialist chairman and Swedish prime minister after 23 years in office; he was succeeded by Palme who at 42 was Europe's youngest head of government. In domestic policies the Social Democrats continued the implementation of their new economic program, seeking with the creation of a ministry of industry and other reforms to promote their proclaimed socioeconomic objectives.

With the approach of the 1970 election—the first to Sweden's new unicameral legislature—nonsocialist leaders and the Left Party-Communists responded to Socialist policies with themes of attack that were similar to those in the preceding two campaigns. Charging that the new economic program would increase the concentration of political authority in the hands of a single party, nonsocialist forces extended their *Borgfreden* in a common effort to displace the Social Democrats from cabinet office. As in 1966 and 1968, however, only the Liberals and the Center Party issued a joint campaign program. The Left Party-Communists suffered marginally from internal strife when a Maoist faction split off to form the Marxist-Leninist Communist Association, but Hermansson retained the loyalty of most radical left supporters in the party's agitation for more extensive socialization measures than the Social Democrats were willing to contemplate.

Discontent over rising prices and inflation, combined with Palme's difficulty in establishing an image comparable in popular appeal to that of Erlander, yielded a Socialist decline in September 1970 that was reminiscent of the party's defeat in 1966. Socialist strength fell to 45.3 percent, with losses occurring to both the right and the left. Aggregate nonsocialist support rose to 47.6 percent, although only the Liberals and the Center increased their share of the popular vote (to 16.2 and 19.9 percent, respectively). Moderate Unity party strength declined to 11.5 percent as former conservative voters who strongly favored intensified nonsocialist cooperation apparently switched their allegiance to one of the middle parties. Abetted by fading public memories of the 1968 Soviet invasion of Czechoslovakia, the Left Party-Communists advanced to 4.8 percent. Their Marxist-Leninist rivals amassed only 0.4 percent.

As a result, the Social Democrats lost their previous absolute majority in parliament. They remained the largest single party with 163 seats in the new Riksdag, but they confronted a bloc of 170 nonsocialist deputies. Accordingly the 17 Left Party-Communist delegates assumed pivotal significance. As a nonsocialist coalition was impossible because the Social Democrats and Left Party-Communists together claimed 180 seats, Palme was able to retain control of cabinet office for his party with the tacit support of the Hermansson faction. Even though reliance on the Left Party-Communists was politically disconcerting to them, the Social Democrats had no alternative. The day following the election Palme declared: "We shall continue to pursue our policies and will stand or fall on them. . . . At the end of the 1940s there were as many, or more, Communists in the Riksdag. This is neither a new situation nor anything especially frightening for us."[66]

PARTIES AND SYSTEM TRANSFORMATION

The 1960s thus revealed a continuing transition of the Swedish multiparty system with respect to both the concentration of parties and attitudes toward system change. Structurally, the most apparent transformation concerned the nonsocialist parties. Widespread popular endorsement of welfare state principles and the persistence of Social Democratic executive leadership constituted the principal causes of increased bloc cohesion. Similar tendencies can be noted in other advanced European systems, with the mutual acceptance of comprehensive welfare services mitigating earlier forms of ideological cleavages in such countries as Britain and West Germany and long-term Labor (or Social Democratic) rule contributing to the emergence of unified nonsocialist electoral alliances and coalition governments in Norway and Denmark.

Although the formal coordination of electoral programs in

[66] *Dagens Nyheter*, September 22, 1970, p. 5.

Sweden was limited initially to the Liberals and the Center, the *Borgfreden* and opposition cooperation in parliament suggested potential precedents for more extensive three-party collaboration in the future. In addition, the adoption of the renamed Moderate Unity party's new program of "humanistic conservatism" in 1969 may provide a partial condition for closer bloc ties by decreasing the ideological distance between the Conservatives and the two middle parties. Nevertheless important barriers to achieving a positive synthesis of nonsocialist policies remain in the form of personal rivalries among the three leaders and the inherent difficulties of coordinating disparate party organizations. If such obstacles can be overcome, the result would be the transformation of the present party system into a functional two-party system dominated by the Social Democrats and a united nonsocialist bloc.

Shifts in political attitudes toward system change resulted from the effects of multiple forms of the new political radicalism on party ideologies and the ebb and flow of electoral fortunes. In part the nonsocialist gains in 1966 and 1970, as well as the increased interest among nonsocialist leaders in intensified nonsocialist cooperation, can be attributed to the agitation among younger Liberal, Center, and to a lesser extent Conservative activists for a positive program of sociopolitical reform. The influence of the New Left on ideological renewal was even more direct, prompting the victory of revisionist forces within the Communist party that led to the resurgence of Communist electoral strength. Confronted with the increased competitiveness of a partially consolidated nonsocialist bloc and the New Left ideological critique of their government policies, the Social Democrats modified their own attitudes toward system change by undertaking new socioeconomic policy initiatives.

One largely unanticipated consequence of the dialectics of party change has been the increased importance of the nation's youth as a political resource. Because of the traditional function of party youth organizations as sources of political recruitment, established leaders could ill afford to discount emerging discontent among younger members over such questions as intraparty democracy and social reform. Moreover, prevailing elite predispositions to respect opposing viewpoints encouraged a conciliatory attitude toward dissidents within party ranks. Hence Sweden's political leaders have made a determined effort to appease younger party members by elevating them to positions of authority. For example, the Liberals elected Per Ahlmark, one of the most outspoken advocates of nonsocialist renewal, as a full member of the party executive committee in 1964, and the Social Democrats bypassed older candidates for the party chairmanship in selecting Palme as Prime Minister Erlander's successor. All of the parties have also sought to broaden their appeal to younger voters, concentrating much of their efforts during the 1968 and 1970 campaigns on the various party youth organizations in an attempt to court first-time voters.

The long-range result of various manifestations of change in the Swedish party system may be to hasten broader processes of postindustrial transformation. Increased bloc competitiveness would facilitate—whichever party or coalition is in office—a dynamic policy synthesis between the Socialist emphasis on collective measures to achieve greater equality and nonsocialist aspirations to maximize the potential for individual choice.

SIX
THE NEW PLURALISM
Groups and system transformation

Alongside political parties, interest groups play a prominent role in all modern pluralist societies as representative organizations seeking to aggregate particular socioeconomic strata and promoting policy decisions on behalf of their special clientele. Distinguished from political parties because they do not usually attempt to gain direct control of public office, interest groups characteristically "bring power to bear where it will produce intended consequences"[1] by participating in formal and informal processes of policy formation. Thus they may apply selective pressure within the executive-administrative apparatus, cultivate contacts with members of political parties and legislative bodies, and/or negotiate directly with their counterparts outside the formal structures of government.

Organized interests in the industrialized, complex welfare states of Scandinavia are no exception. By virtue of their numerical strength, economic resources, and status as national structures of social mobilization and integration, they comprise a major component in what Rokkan describes as a "two-tiered system of decision-making."[2] While elections determine the composition of

[1] Harry Eckstein, *Pressure Group Politics* (Stanford, Calif.: Stanford University Press, 1960), p. 20.

[2] Stein Rokkan, "Norway: Numerical Democracy and Corporate Pluralism," in Robert A. Dahl (ed.), *Political Oppositions in Western Democracies* (New Haven, Conn.: Yale University Press, 1966), p. 107.

parliament and the executive decides national policy guidelines, the major interest groups exercise important "corporate bargaining" functions in their own right. In the particular case of Sweden they have "contributed to the manifest stability of modern . . . society . . . [and] constitute a type of power balance . . . that is of an entirely different sort than the balance of power found in the written constitution."[3]

The principal significance of organized interests in Sweden lies in their autonomous role on the labor market and their supportive-bargaining links with the political system. As countervailing powers to political and administrative decision makers, they are fundamental elements in the institutionalized pluralism of Sweden's industrial-welfare state. Like the political parties, they, too, have been affected by the radical debate of the 1960s—with important implications for the future of pluralism itself.

ORGANIZED INTERESTS: MEMBERSHIP AND STRUCTURE

Most organized interests in Sweden correspond to Almond and Powell's definition of associational interest groups as those manifesting "explicit representation of the interests of a particular group, a full-time professional staff, and orderly procedures for the formulation of interests and demands."[4] The most important in the policy process are the economic interest groups. Based on specialized productive-distributive interests, the major economic groups are the labor, white-collar, business, and agricultural associations and the cooperative movement. A second type of associational interest group in Sweden is the promotional or "idealistic" association which typically recruits members from diverse social strata. Leading examples are the various temperance societies. Whereas organized religion functions as a promotional interest group in many nations, this is not wholly the case in Sweden. The central government exercises direct administrative authority over ecclesiastical activities, appointing church officials and establishing guidelines for religious instruction in schools. Only the free churches are autonomous, but their interaction with political actors appears minimal. The emphasis in this chapter is on the first of these two principal types of interest groups.

[3] Andrén, *Svensk statskunskap* (Stockholm: Bokförlaget Liber, 1963), pp. 34–35.

[4] Gabriel Almond and G. Bingham Powell, Jr., *Comparative Politics. A Developmental Approach* (Boston: Little, Brown and Company, 1966), p. 78.

Parallel with the rise of political parties, organized interest groups emerged as products of economic and social modernization. Some associations were founded to promote the interests of new social strata (such as industrial and white-collar workers), others to protect those of a declining stratum (such as the farmers). Alternatively, some organizations were formed in response to the prior organization of another group, as was the case with employers who forged the Swedish Employers' Association (SAF) in 1902 after the Swedish Federation of Labor (LO) had been established in 1898. With the progressive transformation of Sweden into an advanced industrial-welfare system, the major economic interest groups have increased in national importance as cohesive mass-based structures exercising significant economic and political functions.

From an initial membership of several hundred workers organized solely in local unions, the LO has evolved into a highly centralized national association that encompasses over 90 percent of the nation's industrial work force. Its economic counterpart, the SAF, underwent simultaneous processes of structural centralization, and functions today as the national spokesman of over 25,000 individual firms. Nearly a quarter of the member companies in SAF are also represented in Sweden's Federation of Industries.

White-collar workers were slower to organize than either of the two major partners in the labor market because of "a persistent attitude among salaried employees, in public as well as private service, that they should identify with their employers."[5] But the refusal of employers to provide adequate compensation for the effects of inflation during World War I and the sheer increase in the number of white-collar workers—approximately 250 percent between 1930 and 1956—prompted a change in group consciousness. In 1931 salaried employees in private industry formed the first national white-collar union (DACO), while those in national and communal administrations organized their own association (TCO) in 1937. The two groups merged in 1947 as the Central Organization of Salaried Employees (TCO). A second national white-collar union, made up of civil servants, was organized in 1946 as the Federation of Government Employees (SR). Persons with academic degrees—including teachers and doctors—joined in 1947 to form a third white-collar association, the Swedish Con-

---

[5] Nils Elvander, *Intresseorganisationerna i dagens Sverige* (Lund: CWK Gleerup Bokförlag, 1966), p. 4.

federation of Professional Associations (SACO). Together TCO, SR, and SACO represent nearly all middle and higher level salaried employees; approximately 300,000 lower level white-collar workers are members of the LO.

Within the agricultural sector the primary form of organization is an extensive network of cooperatives which include such groups as the Swedish Meat Producers Society, the Agrarian Loan Association, the Wheat Producers Society, the Farmers' National Association, and the Forestry Owners National Association.[6] In recent decades two national unions, the RLF (the National Associations of Farmers) and the SL (the Swedish Farmers Association) have functioned as central instruments of political agitation. They merged in 1971 to form a unified National Association of Farmers.

The Swedish Cooperative Association (KF) was founded in 1899 as a loose confederation of local consumer societies with an initial membership of 10,000. The KF grew rapidly in size and strength, increasing its membership to more than 400,000 by the 1920s and initiating its own production in competition with private enterprise. In 1966 annual KF sales totaled over five and a half million crowns. Similar to the LO and the SAF, the cooperative movement has experienced a continuing trend toward centralization. As the national organization has grown in strength, the local societies have decreased both in number and autonomous authority.[7]

Membership totals of the nine major economic interest groups (with data from 1945 as a base of comparison) are shown in Table 11.

The largest promotional interest groups are the temperance societies. Organized into eight national associations with 6246 local chapters, Sweden's prohibitionists numbered 377,121 in 1967—a decline from 402,225 two years previously. In addition, 313,051 Swedes are members of 11 dissenting religious sects.

All of the major economic interest groups embody a broadly similar pattern of hierarchical structure. Each is organized on representative principles, with appointed or elected delegates, for example, from local societies or unions or from individual business firms, attending periodic congresses to debate and generally acclaim group policies. Between conventions small executive

---

[6] The total membership of Sweden's 14 agricultural cooperations in 1968 was 977,400, down from 1,025,100 members in 1961. *Statistisk årsbok 1968*, p. 102.

[7] Between 1965 and 1966 the number of cooperative societies declined from 338 to 197. *Statistisk årsbok 1968*, p. 143.

Table 11   Membership in Sweden's Principal Economic
Interest Groups

Association	Membership 1945[a]	1967[b]
LO	1,106,900	1,607,077
SAF	7,890[c]	35,831 (1968)
Federation of Industries	2,440[c]	
TCO	104,650	504,861
SACO	15,000 (1947)	98,720
SR	18,100 (1946)	18,000
RLF	154,340	157,139
SL	365,003	1,047,000[d]
KF	827,790	1,355,834[e](1966)

[a]Nils Elvander, *Intresseorganisationerna i dagens Sverige* (Lund:CWK Gleerup Bokförlag, 1966), p. 49.
[b]*Statistisk årsbok 1968.*
[c]Member firms.
[d]An inflated estimate because of simultaneous membership in several branch organizations.
[e]In addition, 52,285 were members of independent consumer cooperatives (1966).

bodies, which range in size from 10 members in the TCO to 30 in the Federation of Industries, conduct the day-to-day affairs of the association.[8]

In negotiations on the labor market, as in their relations with political parties and government authorities, the objective strength of organized economic interest groups in Sweden (measured in terms of membership and internal cohesion) provides the basic condition of their effectiveness as direct participants in decision processes.

THE LABOR MARKET

In contrast to other modern systems where the national government has intervened to force wage agreements on recalcitrant negotiating partners (as has occurred periodically in the United States and Great Britain), labor market relations in Sweden are virtually free of direct government interference. Comprehensive legislation affecting management and labor exists in the form of laws governing mediation in labor conflicts (1906 and 1920), collective agreements and the Labor Court (1928), and freedom

8 Elvander, *Intresseorganisationerna*, pp. 48–68.

of association and negotiation (1936). Primary responsibility for regulating the nonpublic sector of the economy is delegated, however, almost wholly to the LO and the SAF. It is accordingly within the labor market that Sweden's economic interest groups contribute an important direct influence on national policy.

The relatively passive role of the Swedish government with respect to management-labor relations results largely from the joint determination of the LO and the SAF "to solve their own problems."[9] Although the first decades of the century were marked by continual strikes and retaliatory lockouts, the LO and SAF reached a *modus vivendi* by the 1930s in which each party accepted the other as an equal. One impetus was provided by the collective agreements act of 1928 which constrained labor and management from resorting to open conflict if a dispute between a particular union and a company involved the interpretation of a given collective wage agreement. Instead such disputes were to be settled by the Labor Court, which consisted originally of two members from the LO and two from the SAF plus three nonpartisans, all of whom are appointed by the government.[10] On their own initiative, the LO and the SAF undertook the most significant move in regulating the labor market when they signed the historic "Saltsjöbaden Agreement" (named after the resort town on the east coast at which it was negotiated) in 1938. The pact, which provides the framework for contemporary relations between the LO and the SAF, "established negotiation procedures including grievance procedure; rules which must be observed in case of dismissals and lay-offs; limitations on strikes, lockouts and similar direct action; and a special procedure applying to conflicts jeopardizing vital interests of the community."[11]

Under terms of the Saltsjöbaden Agreement the LO and the SAF have implemented regular bargaining procedures as autonomous actors responsible for maintaining Sweden's wage stabilization policies and labor peace. The government's role is restricted to that of mediator in cases of extended disagreement. A wage freeze imposed during World War II remained largely in force through the initial postwar years, but from 1952 onward the national leadership of the LO and SAF initiated central negotiations on nationwide package wage agreements. Conducted on an annual

[9] Elvander, *Intresseorganisationerna*, p. 99.
[10] A representative of the TCO was added to the Labor Court in 1947. Since 1966 a government representative replaced one of the SAF delegates, when a dispute involves the state as employer.
[11] Swedish Trade Union Confederation, *Landsorganisationen i Sverige* (Stockholm: Tiden, 1964), p. 18.

basis until 1956 and for two-year intervals until 1966, the LO-SAF negotiations now determine recommendations on wages, working hours, and fringe benefits for periods of three years. The national agreements serve as the basis for formal contract negotiations between the unions and companies affiliated with the LO and the SAF, respectively. In reality, their effect is national in scope, for "all other categories of private and public employees base their wage demands on [the LO-SAF] recommendation."[12] Thus negotiations between the white-collar unions—representing teachers and other professional workers—and private employers as well as the state are guided by previous decisions between the two major partners on the labor market.

Underlying the willingness of LO and SAF leaders to cooperate in positive efforts to sustain long-term economic stability and growth are shared attitudes that extend beyond narrow group claims. Speaking in behalf of the role of the LO in contemporary Swedish society, a committee composed of prominent union officials asserted in 1966:

> It is apparent to us that an important source of strength of the trade union movement . . . has been its determination and ability to adjust its organization and activities to social change. An interest group that limits itself to the protection of existing group interests runs the risk of becoming ossified in tradition and losing its influence over [socioeconomic] developments. If, on the other hand, an organization accepts change and can integrate its group interests within general processes of development, . . . the organization has an opportunity to take active part in shaping the future.[13]

From the perspective of private enterprise, Axel Iveroth, chairman of the Federation of Industries, has described the "industrial interest" of business groups in Sweden as "an effort to maintain the most advantageous possible milieu for industrial production. Through extrapolation one can say that our ultimate goal is to achieve a socioeconomic organization that enables all those who live and work here to benefit as much as possible from 'the good life.' "[14]

The contributions of the LO and the SAF to labor peace

---

[12] *Landsorganisationen i Sverige*, p. 15.

[13] *Fackföreningsrörelsen och den tekniska utvecklingen. Rapport från en arbetsgrupp till 1966 års LO-kongress* (Stockholm: Bokförlaget Prisma, 1966), p. 15.

[14] Axel Iveroth, "Industriförbundets verksamhetsformer," concluding remarks at the Falsterbo conference on September 10, 1963 (Stockholm: Sveriges industriförbund, 1966), p. 1. (Mimeographed.)

have been significant. Since 1955 the number of official work stoppages has been uniformally low, with most wage disputes yielding to compromise settlements between labor and management. (See Table 12.) In broader perspective the functional responsibilities of the two major partners in the labor market have

Table 12   Work Stoppages, 1955–1969[a]

| Year | Work Stoppages | | Working Days Lost (in 1000s) |
	Total	Of which Strikes	
1955	18	18	159
1956	12	12	4
1957	20	19	53
1958	10	9	15
1959	17	16	24
1960	31	29	18
1961	12	12	2
1962	10	10	5
1963	24	23	25
1964	14	14	34
1965	8	8	14
1966	26	25	352[b]
1967	7	7	0[c]
1968	7	7	1
1969	32	31	112

| Year | Outcome of Disputes | | |
	Settled on Management Terms	Settled on Labor Terms	Compromise, Indecisive
1955			18
1956	3	1	8
1957	3		17
1958		1	9
1959	6	1	10
1960	6	11	14
1961		6	6
1962	5	1	4
1963	13	1	10
1964	6		8
1965	4		4
1966	6	5	15
1967	1	1	5
1968	2	1	4
1969	24	1	7

[a]*Statistisk årsbok för Sverige* (Stockholm: Statistiska centralbyrån, 1970), p. 236. Hereafter referred to as *Statistisk årsbok 1970.*
[b]This total is accounted for largely by a nationwide teacher's strike in the fall of the year.
[c]Only 400 working days were lost.

proved of decisive importance "not only for the organization and their relations with the government, but also for the formulation and performance of Swedish democracy. Here has been created a condition of freedom under responsibility, of stability and order. . . ."[15]

INTEREST GROUPS, POLITICAL PARTIES, AND THE RIKSDAG

Beyond their direct role in regulating labor market relations, all of the leading organized economic associations attempt through multiple political channels to affect policy decisions favorable to their particular interests. Because of the high correlation between socioeconomic differentiation and electoral preferences, political parties and their representatives in parliament provide natural access routes for the promotion of group goals. The significance of parties and parliament as sites of group participation in political processes varies in proportion to degrees of party-group alignment and party or bloc cohesiveness in the Riksdag.

The strongest alignment exists between the LO and the Social Democratic party. Representing complementary economic and political facets of the working-class movement, both organizations have from the outset emphasized their close ideological and interest affinity. Although there are no institutionalized bonds between the LO and the Social Democrats, the same personnel have often occupied leading positions in both structures. A prominent illustration is Arne Geijer, the present chairman of the LO, who serves as one of seven full members on the Social Democratic Executive Committee. Moreover, the LO contributes 60 to 70 percent of the party membership through the collective affiliation of individual unions and provides the principal source of the party's financial resources. In 1964, for example, the LO and member unions donated 4,144,500 crowns to Social Democratic campaign efforts.[16] LO and party members also form joint *ad hoc* committees to coordinate campaign strategy, with union mobilization of voters contributing a substantial share of Socialist electoral support. Within parliament 45 members of the Social Democratic delegation in 1963–1965 were either members of the LO or party members who considered themselves spokesmen for organized labor.[17]

Given the majority status of the Social Democrats in the Riksdag and their long-term control of cabinet office, the LO is

---

[15] Elvander, *Intresseorganisationerna*, p. 29.
[16] Elvander, *Intresseorganisationerna*, p. 148.
[17] Elvander, *Intresseorganisationerna*, p. 148.

able to utilize its extensive horizontal and vertical links with the Socialists to play an active part in formulating government economic and social policies. Important instances of LO-Social Democratic policy collaboration include the supplementary pension program of 1959 and the new economic program of 1968.

The cooperative movement has also been traditionally aligned with the Social Democrats. Most KF deputies in parliament are Social Democrats, and all parliamentary activity on behalf of KF interests is channeled through the majority party.

Relations between Sweden's other interest groups and political parties are more diffused. Employer groups within the SAF and the Federation of Industries concede that they contribute financially to both the Moderate Unity and the Liberal parties.[18] Similarly the National Association of Farmers provides considerable manpower and financial support for the Center. But all three interest associations as well as the TCO, SACO, and SR claim official "neutrality" in their political orientations, and seek to influence the democratic parties simultaneously.

One measure of the absence of concentrated group-party ties among nonlabor forces is the distribution of interests association representation among various Riksdag delegations. In the period 1963–1965 members of SACO, RLF, and SL were dispersed among all four democratic parliamentary factions; members of TCO and SR were in the Moderate Unity, Liberal, and Social Democratic parties; and members of the SAF and the Federation of Industries served in the three nonsocialist parties.[19]

Because of the fragmentation of the nonsocialist bloc, leaders of interest associations that identify most clearly with the individualist assumptions of nonsocialist ideology, in particular employer organizations and some groups within the white-collar unions, accord parties and parliamentary representation relatively less attention than does the LO. Communications between economic interests and nonsocialist political spokesmen are intermittent, and usually are undertaken on the initiative of party leaders. Occasionally interest organizations provide information and expertise at the behest of the nonsocialist parties (especially the Moderate Unity party).[20] But, as Iveroth maintains, the "research sections

[18] Gunnar Heckscher, "Interest Groups in Sweden: Their Political Role," in Henry W. Ehrmann (ed.), *Interest Groups on Four Continents* (Pittsburgh, Pa.: University of Pittsburgh Press, 1958), p. 163.

[19] Elvander, *Intresseorganisationerna*, p. 198.

[20] Elvander reports that 46 percent of the Conservative deputies he interviewed affirmed that they had received material from economic associations (compared to 25 percent of Liberal and Center parliamentarians). *Intresseorganisationerna*, p. 205.

of the [economic] associations are so inundated by their own work that they can offer only limited assistance to the political parties."[21]

A very different situation characterizes relations between organized interest groups and the formal political-administrative apparatus. Institutionalized and informal provisions for extensive consultations between the government and established economic organizations during the circulatory (or preparliamentary) stage of legislation and membership in various administrative boards provide interest groups their most decisive avenues for interaction with political authorities.

ROYAL COMMISSIONS AND <u>REMISS</u> PROCEDURES

The two principal forums of direct interest group participation in deliberations on specific policy proposals are Royal Commissions and elaborate *remiss* (consultative) procedures. Both serve as important means of consultation (as opposed to negotiation) between organized interests and decision makers, and both allow the government to elicit as wide a range of views as possible before it formally commits itself to a particular policy initiative.[22]

Royal Commissions, which originated in the nineteenth century, are committees of investigation appointed by the cabinet or individual ministers to gather facts on specific issues and recommend legislative action. The impetus for a Royal Commission may arise either within the government or from an administrative agency, members or committees in parliament, or an interest group. Once appointed, a Royal Commission conducts its investigations independently of the government. A commission's final report is usually accepted by the government as the basis for its own policy proposal in parliament.

Originally recruited entirely from the civil service and the political parties, Royal Commissions gradually broadened their

[21] Axel Iveroth, "Die Rolle der Politik in der schwedischen Wirtschaft," speech at the Politisches Seminar der Staatsbürgerlichen Gesellschaft in Bad Godesberg on October 21, 1964 (Stockholm: Sveriges Industriförbund, 1964), p. 9. (Mimeographed.)

[22] Eckstein distinguishes between negotiations and consultations as follows: "Negotiations take place when a governmental body makes a decision hinging upon the actual approval of organizations interested in it, giving the organizations a veto over the decision; consultations occur when the views of the organizations are solicited and taken into account, but not considered to be in any sense decisive." Eckstein, p. 23.

membership from the 1930s onward to include representatives of Sweden's leading interest associations. By the period from 1935 to 1944, Meijer reports, the percentage of organization membership exceeded that of political parties. Organizations clearly dominated over party representation from 1945 to 1954; since then the percentage of interest group and party membership has been approximately equal.[23]

Initially associations such as the SAF and LO participated in Royal Commission deliberations that dealt only with their specialized interests. However, as organized groups have grown in strength, and as their percentage of commission membership has increased, they have increasingly taken part in "matters outside the original purview of the group. General economic policy, social policy, trade policy and education are fields that have often been investigated by commissions composed of representatives of employers, labor unions, and other economic organizations and cultural or religious associations."[24] Organizations have justified their involvement in such broad areas of policy on the grounds that "economic questions cannot be isolated from their sociopolitical context, for the actual standard of living among group members is affected by a wider range of factors than nominal increases in wages."[25]

The capacity of interest groups to influence political decisions through their participation in Royal Commissions is a function of the deliberative style of most commissions and the effect of commission reports on subsequent government policy. In the first place members attempt, even though they are formally independent of instructions from their particular association, to achieve compromise decisions based on the various group viewpoints represented on the commission. As Gunnar Heckscher writes: "The tendency is to attempt the greatest possible amount of agreement already at this stage, since proposals can more easily be carried if the commission has been unanimous."[26] Second, the recommendations of a Royal Commission often effectively bind the government to a given course of action. The attitudes of interest groups (as well as political parties) on Royal Commissions restrict "to a considerable degree the government's range of [pol-

---

[23] See Table 20 in Chapter Eight.

[24] Hans Meijer, *Kommitépolitik och kommitéarbete* (Lund: CWK Gleerup Bokförlag, 1956), pp. 351–352.

[25] Hans Wieslander, "Organisationerna i det moderna samhället," in Pär-Erik Back (ed.), *Modern Demokrati*, 2d ed., rev. (Lund: CWK Gleerup Bokförlag, 1965), p. 192.

[26] Heckscher, "Interest Groups in Sweden," p. 166.

icy] choice. By defining points of view and often limiting choices for later consideration, the commission system occupies a central position in the decision-making process."[27]

Complementing Royal Commissions as a formal channel of interest group participation in the deliberative process is the *remiss* system of consultation. The Swedish constitution expressly requires ministers to obtain information from appropriate administrative agencies before an issue is brought before the King-in-Council; in practice interest associations are invited to submit their views on pending government measures as well. The usual procedure is for a ministerial department to request administrative agencies and organized interests to comment on policy proposals previously submitted by Royal Commissions or within the public administration. When the replies have been received from the public and private groups, they are submitted along with the original documents and the government's own recommendations to the Riksdag for final consideration.

Among the principal interest groups discussed in this chapter, the Federation of Industries is the most active source of *remiss* memoranda. The KF, in contrast, supplied the fewest number of commentaries. (See Table 13.)

The qualitative influence of *remiss* procedures on government policy is difficult to measure. Heckscher maintains that "on the whole the views expressed by organizations such as LO, TCO, SAF, KF, and the farming cooperatives are taken equally or more seriously than those presented by government organizations."[28]

Table 13 Number of *Remiss* Commentaries among Major Interest Associations, 1964[a]

Association	Number
Federation of Industries	108
SACO	91
LO	87
TCO	86
SL	64
SAF	61
RLF	57
KF	57
SR	31

[a]Adapted from Elvander, *Intresseorganisationerna*, p. 86.

[27] Meijer, p. 3.
[28] Heckscher, "Interest Groups in Sweden," p. 166.

Probably a more accurate appraisal, as Lars Foyer suggests, is that "the effect of the *remiss* commentaries by organizations is greatest when they restrict themselves to more technical questions within their specific sphere of activity."[29]

On a significantly more informal level, interest groups also regularly interact with various government agencies in the daily deliberative and administrative process. Nils Elvander has found that "these contacts assume the most varied forms and frequency, ranging from almost daily telephone conversations among salaried employees [in government and private service] who exchange specialized information and control technical data to regular consultations at the highest level in important political questions."[30] The groups claiming the highest number of such informal contacts are the SAF, TCO, and LO—in that order.[31]

ADMINISTRATIVE RESPONSIBILITIES

In addition to their participatory role in the various circulatory stages of legislation, organized interests exercise direct administrative responsibilities as semiofficial political actors. Although such functions are limited in scope, they contribute to the legitimization of an active role by interest groups in Swedish political processes.

Within the national administrative structure, representatives of economic associations are members of approximately 20 government agencies with advisory and in some cases, decision-making powers. One of the most important such organs, cited above, is the Labor Court. Other examples include the Labor Market Board, which oversees general measures to sustain full employment; the administration boards of the National Pensions' Board and the supplementary pension fund; and (with advisory status) such agencies as the Traffic Safety Board and the Oil Protection Board.[32]

The leading illustration of direct delegation of administrative authority to interest groups is within the agrarian sector of the

29 Lars Foyer, "Former för kontakt och samverkan mellan staten och organisationerna," in Sweden, Justitiedepartementet, *Statens offentliga utredningar 1961:21, Författningsutredningen: V, Organisationer, Beslutsteknik, Valsystem* (Stockholm: Justitiedepartementet, 1961), p. 17.
30 Elvander, *Intresseorganisationerna*, p. 174.
31 Elvander, *Intresseorganisationerna*, p. 174.
32 Foyer, p. 50.

economy. Beginning in the early 1930s, the central government cooperated with local agrarian societies to transform farmer cooperatives into official price-support agencies. New organizations such as the National Wheat Producers' Association (SMR) were assigned complete responsibility "to regulate prices—in an effort to balance export prices and the domestic price level—in place of the government."[33] Additional associations, composed of representatives of both the agrarian cooperatives and private firms, were created under government aegis to administer price supports in such areas as meat and dairy production.[34] Subject to policy directives from the national government, the cooperatives and special regulatory associations remain the primary means through which Swedish agricultural policy is administered.

HARPSUND DEMOCRACY

Their extensive functions on the labor market and intricate connections with political and administrative structures on virtually all levels of Swedish government assure organized interests a pivotal role in domestic policy. Through their self-regulation of management-labor relations, the major economic groups have contributed significantly to the stability of long-term processes of socioeconomic change. Formal and informal access to official decision makers provide them comprehensive means to protect—and, if possible, to enhance—the interests of the occupational or social strata whom they represent.

The penetration of organized interests into the political system is by no means without reciprocal advantage for the government. By forcing organizations "to take a position at an early state in actual questions, "membership on Royal Commissions and participation in *remiss* procedures can induce group leaders to "become morally bound to accept loyally government measures in the future."[35] In addition, consultations between organized interests and political-administrative personnel "provide the government an excellent opportunity to obtain expertise and knowledge about [public] opinion."[36]

In light of long-term Social Democratic control of cabinet office, the major beneficiary of the highly developed contacts be-

[33] Elvander, *Intresseorganisationerna*, p. 40.
[34] Foyer, p. 69.
[35] Foyer, p. 11.
[36] Wieslander, "Organisationerna i det moderna samhället," p. 195.

tween private and public authorities has been the LO. Not only have leaders of organized labor collaborated with the Social Democrats in sponsoring major postwar policy innovations such as the new economic program, they have also proved instrumental in prompting the government to undertake given measures over the objections of other groups. A case in point was the cabinet's decision in 1965 to postpone consideration of proposed tax reform legislation, which had previously been endorsed by business and white-collar interests, in response to LO criticism during the *remiss* stage of consultation.[37]

Other groups have succeeded in achieving their own degree of rapport with the Social Democrats, however, as a result of a discernible trend toward intensified top-level contacts between organized interests and members of the government. The very persistence of Socialist executive leadership has encouraged associations such as the SAF and the Federation of Industries to seek a *rapprochement* with the majority party, even at the risk of weakening their nominal political spokesmen—the nonsocialist parties —in parliament. Symbolized by the epithet "Harpsund democracy," the institution of regular meetings between organization leaders and cabinet ministers outside established consultative channels seemed to some critical observers to herald the transformation of Sweden's institutionalized pluralism into functional corporativism.

Since 1939 the government has periodically invited representatives of business interests to confer on economic and financial questions. Contacts were extended in 1949 when government and business leaders initiated informal talks to consider means to expand production and reduce unemployment, but they were gradually abandoned after several years.[38] In 1959 similar sessions were resumed, this time at the prime minister's weekend residence at Harpsund just outside of Stockholm, at the mutual agreement of labor, business, and Socialist spokesmen.

The ostensible purpose of the Harpsund consultations, which quickly became known as Harpsund democracy, was for organizations and cabinet officials to exchange information prior to the formation of important economic legislation. Because members of the nonsocialist parties were excluded from the meetings, critics (including some within the Social Democratic party) considered

[37] Elvander, *Intresseorganisationerna*, p. 254.
[38] The group, known as the "Thursday club" after the day on which it regularly met, had a floating membership of approximately 70 persons. Foyer, p. 18.

the private talks between groups and government a potential threat to Swedish democracy.[39] Nonsocialist leaders charged that Harpsund democracy led to extraparliamentary agreements that were subsequently "rubber-stamped" by the Socialist majority in the Riksdag, with their own ability to influence decisions on Royal Commissions and in parliament reduced proportionately.

In a censorious editorial *Dagens Nyheter* asserted that "parliament is in reality relegated to the sidelines, even if a bill in question is formally deliberated by the normal political organs." It is of historical record, the paper noted, that the LO had traditionally exerted an influence on Social Democratic policies; "but the new development that is taking place is that organizations and interest groups which do not have political connections with the Social Democrats are increasingly favoring direct contact with the government rather than openly making known their demands and wishes in public debate."[40]

A secretary of the Liberal party stated privately that "it is good for parties and the government to confer with organizations. What we criticize at Harpsund are those questions that have been decided there. The government must be free to act and cannot be bound. Yet it is bound in that the discussions come close to being decisions." Similarly a Conservative spokesman condemned Harpsund democracy on the ground that "the Conservative party is strongly opposed to agreements reached outside parliament." Echoing the Liberal party attitude, a leading official in the Center party stated that "the government should not be hindered in contacting interest groups, but there should be no binding decisions."[41]

Business and labor participants at the meetings were unanimous in denying that actual decisions were made that pledged the government and organizations to a definite policy commitment. An official of the Federation of Industries stated that "there have never been any negotiations at Harpsund" and that the primary purpose of the consultations was merely to discuss pending problems. LO leaders also disclaimed knowledge of any Harpsund decisions between organized interests and the cabinet.[42] Nevertheless one close observer reported that former Prime Minister

---

[39] Nils Elvander, "Organisationerna och statsmakterna," *Industriförbundets tidskrift*, 8 (October 1963), 424–429.

[40] *Dagens Nyheter*, October 16, 1963, p. 2.

[41] Private interviews with party officials.

[42] Private interviews with employer and LO representatives.

Erlander recalled at least two agreements that were reached at Harpsund: one concerning credit grants to small business firms and a second relating to the regulation of insurance savings. He quotes Finance Minister Gunnar Sträng as saying, "We'll be able to arrange that."[43]

Although opposition fears concerning the emergence of an incipient corporativism were undoubtedly exaggerated, the Harpsund deliberations were indicative of the growing stature of organized interests as recognized partners in decision processes. The meetings were subsequently discontinued, largely in response to press criticism, but functional equivalents have been created in the form of the Research Council and the Planning Board (established in 1962. The former is designed to coordinate basic research on problems of industrial development, while the latter serves as an advisory group to the government to consider long-term economic and investment planning. Representatives of the LO, SAF, Federation of Industries, TCO, and KF are members of both structures. The government is represented on the Planning Board by members of the ministries of Finance, Trade, Commerce, and Transportation.

Yet the finely tuned balance of pluralist forces that had been attained in the mid-1960s began to undergo significant change by the beginning of the 1970s. Nationally the rise of the New Left had initiated a critical reappraisal of existing group-government relations. By responding to their 1966 electoral defeat with the new economic program of 1968, the Social Democrats instigated a policy shift toward greater social influence over productive resources. Within the associations themselves a reaction among rank-and-file members against highly centralized leadership revealed a deepening malaise with internal characteristics of Sweden's institutionalized pluralism.

The most overt challenge to the principle of group solidarity —the basic condition of effective group participation in economic and political processes—came in the form of a strike from December 1969 to February 1970 in the LKAB mine fields north of the Arctic Circle. Combined with the broader changes affecting the economic system enacted by the Social Democrats, the LKAB strike revealed the outlines of an emerging new pluralism that may characterize groups and group interaction in the future.

[43] Alvar Alsterdal, "Harpsund en synvilla?" *Industria*, 40 (B-edition, 1964), 46.

THE LKAB STRIKE

The setting of the strike was, ironically, not a private company but Sweden's largest public-owned industrial enterprise—the Luosa-vaara-Kiirunavaara AB (LKAB) mining company, which is located approximately 1600 kilometers (nearly 1000 miles) north of Stockholm in Lapland.[44] The company's mines are situated in Kiruna, a city of 25,000 population with an area nearly the size of Connecticut, and adjacent towns of Malmberget and Svappavaara.

Purchased by the national government in 1957, LKAB claims capital resources totaling 1316 million crowns. In 1967 it recorded a turnover of 856 million crowns and employed 6663 persons. Its employees are among the highest paid in Sweden, although differences between their wages and income levels elsewhere in the country have gradually diminished in recent years.

As a government-owned corporation, LKAB has actively promoted LO-Social Democratic concepts of industrial democracy. The company "has pioneered in employee publications, advisory committees and information meetings. Kiruna miners have some of the best fringe benefits in the world. They are transported by bus down an inclined roadway to their place of work. Underground there is two-way bus and car traffic in tunnels with flourescent lights and asphalt surfaces. Nine underground restaurants serve hot meals with beer for about 75 cents, and an area is provided for naps after lunch."[45]

Nevertheless on December 9, 1969, the miners struck. Arguing that wage increases that had recently been negotiated between the Miners Union and LKAB management in accordance with the LO-SAF agreement of 1969 were insufficient, a small group of workers walked off their jobs in Svappavaara. Within days 4700 workers in Svappavaara, Malmberget, and Kiruna were on strike, bringing the LKAB operations to a complete standstill.

Immediate grievances among the workers included demands for higher wages, particularly for older men, who were forced to accept jobs above the ground at a loss in their previous incomes; a monthly pay scale in place of payment for piece work; and the dismissal of certain management officials. Far more significant, however, were the underlying causes of employee discontent. During a decade in which LKAB had undergone extensive rationaliza-

---

[44] The name of the town is a composite of the Finnish words for the two mountains containing the ore deposits and the Swedish abbreviation (AB) for corporation.

[45] *The New York Times*, January 8, 1970, p. 2.

tion, reducing its personnel 17 percent while doubling production, workers had experienced cumulative stress and depersonalization.[46] Adding to their frustration was the failure of the Miners Union to respond to their particular needs. Although the miners in Kiruna and Malmberget comprise half of the union's membership, they are allocated only a quarter of the seats at the union congress.[47] Repeatedly their petitions for better wages and improved employee-employer relations had been ignored by the highly centralized and remote union bureaucracy.

In broader perspective, therefore, the strike "was aimed less against the employers than against the trade unions. Or rather, it was aimed at the bureaucracy that has grown up around the trade unions, a gesture of irritation with an ossifying labor market falling into the hands of officials estranged from the rank and file."[48] By rejecting the union's wage settlement and engaging in what both Swedish law and the Saltsjöbaden Agreement defined as an illegal strike, the workers at LKAB openly repudiated basic tenets of group solidarity. Their action symbolized the potential distintegration of organized labor as a viable sociopolitical force.

Eminent Swedish analysts promptly perceived the deeper causes of the LKAB walkout. Kurt Samuelsson, a leading economic historian and director of the Stockholm Graduate School of Social Work, observed shortly after the strike began: "The price for the great benefits of centralization . . . has been an ever-increasing distance between the leadership and the members, an increasing feeling that all decisions are made centrally, over the heads of the members, that too little is done to cope with the many various local problems which naturally are closest to the individual member."[49] Writing in the Socialist theoretical journal, *Tiden*, Walter Korpi argued that the LKAB strike was not merely the result of special conditions prevailing within a particular union. "The situation within the Miners Union reflects a more general situation that exists in varying degrees throughout the entire labor movement. One could describe it as a crisis of the contemporary form of organized labor."[50] A major symptom of that crisis, he asserted, is that "members feel themselves powerless

[46] Walter Korpi, "Varför strejkar arbetarna?" *Tiden*, 62 (February 1970), 74–75.

[47] Korpi, pp. 75–76.

[48] Roland Huntford, "Why Did They Strike?" *Sweden Now*, 4 (June 1970), 36.

[49] Kurt Samuelsson, "The Ironminers Walkout—Signal of Change?" *Viewpoint* (New York: Swedish Information Service, January 28, 1970), p. 3. (Mimeographed.)

[50] Korpi, p. 75.

within their association and far removed from the union leadership. Union centralization has gone a long way [in Sweden]. The roots of the crisis are probably to be found there."[51]

Official union leaders confronted a dilemma in their attempt to settle the strike. Antipathetic to the union in the first place, the workers had formed their own strike committee and demanded the right to negotiate directly with the LKAB management. If the Miners Union permitted the strike committee to monopolize labor representation at the negotiations, the union would abrogate its own responsibilities on the labor market. Yet the strike had occurred in clear violation of established procedures governing labor market relations. By participating in negotiations the Miners Union would in effect condone an act that conflicted with three decades of joint efforts by the LO and the SAF to maintain labor peace.[52]

The primary necessity of asserting its leadership as the "legitimate" spokesman of labor interests dictated the union's decision. In concert with the LKAB the Miners Union agreed to sanction negotiations. An initial round of discussions was held between company and union officials in Stockholm in early January, but the proposed settlement was rejected by the strike committee in Kiruna. Accordingly the local branch of the union intensified efforts to restore discipline among the striking workers in an attempt to ease the impasse. "And the Swedish trade union movement proved its resilience. It may have become heirarchical, and brought forth a bureaucracy, but it still knew how to agitate."[53]

By mid-January, the union strategy had begun to succeed. A split developed among the strikers, with an increasing number indicating their willingness to resume work on the condition that the LKAB would agree to negotiations in Kiruna.[54] After several hundred workers actually returned to the mines, the strike com-

[51] Korpi, p. 75.

[52] Social Democratic ambivalence toward the strike was apparent in the party press. An editorial on January 9, 1970, in *Aftonbladet*, the largest Socialist paper, stated: "The strike committee has accomplished a good deal by calling attention to a series of injustices. But the strike committee has also demonstrated a total incapacity and an unwillingness to conduct negotiations that can lead to meaningful results." Another Socialist paper, *Arbetarbladet*, observed on January 10, 1970: "Solidarity is a fine characteristic and a source of strength within the labor movement. But to stand together in order to tear apart a legally binding order on the labor market is neither intelligent nor constructive."

[53] Huntford, p. 37.

[54] *Svenska Dagbladet* reported on January 13, 1970, that more than half of the 1000 workers who had attended the most recent mass meeting of the strikers were prepared to return to their jobs.

mittee declared the end of the strike on February 4. Five days later a joint delegation composed of members of the strike committee and the Miners Union opened negotiations with LKAB.

Agreement was reached by the middle of the month. The company consented to increase wages, reduce discrepancies between the lowest and highest income groups, provide monthly salaries rather than piecework wages to the workers, and extend fringe benefits (such as annual recreational allowances) previously reserved to salaried employees to blue-collar workers. Thus the strike was settled largely on the workers' terms. Labor peace was restored, and the Miners Union was able to reestablish control over local representation of miners' interests. But the strike and its outcome raised important implications for the future of group relations in Sweden.

THE NEW PLURALISM

As an empirical manifestation of the tensions accompanying post-industrial modernization, the LKAB strike graphically revealed the inherent contradiction between social norms of efficiency and stability and individual aspirations to attain qualitative improvement in one's immediate environment. From the point of view of the Kiruna miners the centralization of union authority, compounded by the relentless pace of rationalization with the LKAB, negated their effective possibilities to exert a meaningful influence on decisions affecting their work or life conditions. The strike exposed the contradiction to public and elite consciousness, thereby facilitating its possible resolution through appropriate countermeasures by group and political leaders.

Samuelsson has concluded from the events at Kiruna that "rather extensive changes in the structure of the [organized labor] movement will certainly be necessary."[55] His concept of an effective countersystem to existing union organizations—one that conceivably will help reconcile opposing claims of collective and individual control—encompasses improved communications between group leaders and the rank-and-file and the decentralization of negotiating authority to enable local unions to exercise direct influence in deciding local issues. "These changes," he adds, "will also affect which questions are to be regarded as important in the trade union movement, and the priority between them. It will be

[55] Samuelsson, "The Ironminers Walkout," p. 4.

necessary—centrally as well as locally—to pursue more vigorously the problems of the working conditions themselves, that is the social and organizational problems in shops and factories, the industrial democracy."[56]

The LKAB strike suggests simultaneous lessons for employer groups in future negotiations with labor representatives. "Among these lessons are a better understanding of the need for improved industrial psychology, improved internal communications within the enterprises combined with a more open-minded approach to the relations with the employees, and greater caution regarding the position and power of the trade unions. For decades their power has been taken for granted. . . . Now the employers know that this can no longer be taken for granted."[57]

Ultimately, however, problems of bureaucratization and lack of communication (within unions as well as between the unions and employer interests) cannot be solved simply through structural innovations that leave existing power relations among various social strata intact. From the authoritative perspective of the Socialist journal, *Tiden*, "the LKAB conflict may later be viewed as an important positive turning point for the Swedish working-class movement. [This will be the case] if the SAP and the trade unions view it as a symptom of shortcomings in capitalist society and permit it to inspire an energetic effort to reduce class differences by increasing political and union activity [to diminish] differences in incomes, differences in working conditions, and differences in influence and power at places of work. Industrial democracy and economic democracy must be translated into concrete actions."[58]

It is in this context that the Social Democrats' economic program of 1968 assumes its particular significance for the future of groups and group relations in Sweden. Committed to ideological goals of achieving a collective condition of greater equality and security, the Social Democrats have enacted measures to extend social influence on private economic decisions (for example, by appointing government representatives to the boards of companies and banks) and the direct role of the state in the national economy. To implement the latter objective, the Socialists combined the various public corporations in 1969 under a single management in a new ministry of industry and plan to invest with private

---

[56] Samuelsson, p. 4.
[57] Samuelsson, p. 4.
[58] "LKAB-strejkan," *Tiden*, 62 (January 1970), 3.

enterprise in the formation of various joint business ventures. The state-owned Investment Bank, with capital resources of $200,000,000, and the supplementary pension fund, which had grown to $4,456,000,000 by the end of 1969, provide the Swedish government important means to stimulate economic growth in accordance with political priorities.[59]

The new economic program will inevitably affect the distribution of group influence. Even though political leaders do not contemplate the expropriation of private property—on the contrary, they are desirious of even more extensive coordination of socioeconomic policy with private associations than in the past—their efforts to achieve transforming change through more active state intervention in the economy will probably mean a gradual subordination of particular group interests to the larger collectivity.

Hence Sweden's emerging new pluralism embraces both centralizing tendencies, with respect to investments, economic planning, and productive processes, and pressures to decentralize decision making within established groups such as the trade union movement. System transformation that simultaneously allows greater participation by individuals in determining their economic and social existence offers a prospect, but not the certainty, that these contradictory facets of postindustrial modernization can be successfully reconciled.

[59] See David Jenkins, "Mixed Economy," *Sweden Now*, 3 (November 1969), 52–53, 100, 102.

SEVEN
MAJORITY PARLIAMENTARISM
AND POLICY-MAKING ROLES
The structure of government

The significance of formal political structures in modern pluralist systems accrues from their role in defining principal boundaries of interaction among political groups (especially political parties) and providing the central setting for authoritative decisions. According to established parliamentary principles throughout most of Scandinavia, no institutional separation of powers exists between the legislative and executive branches as it does in presidential systems.[1] Instead, comparable to "pure" parliamentary systems like that of Britain, a functional division of authority defines legislative-executive relations. The national parliament serves as the forum from which the executive is recruited and in which government policies are debated and legally ratified; the cabinet exercises primary initiating authority and is accountable to parliament for its actions. Between elections the tenure of a cabinet depends on its ability to maintain majority support based on the numerical strength and cohesion of either a single party or a coalition of parties in the legislative assembly. If such a majority is absent, the inability of opposition forces to agree on the formation of an alternative government may suffice to sustain a minority cabinet in office.

---

[1] Finland and Iceland are qualified exceptions in that a popularly elected president exercises semiautonomous powers in both countries.

A product of modernizing processes in the nineteenth and early twentieth centuries, parliamentarism in Sweden has undergone continual change in both form and substance. The most recent step in structural rationalization was the constitutional reform of 1967–1969 establishing unicameralism. Substantively, the realignment of political forces caused by the rise of the Social Democrats to "permanent" majority status in the early 1930s meant the demise of minority parliamentarism. Subsequent Socialist preeminence has been the decisive factor determining the course of executive-legislative relations into the 1970s.

THE RIKSDAG: ORGANIZATIONS AND FUNCTIONS

The constitutional boundaries of Swedish government are prescribed by two documents: the Instrument of Government (*Regeringsformen*), defining the fundamental basis of parliamentary and executive competence, and the Act of Parliament (*Riksdagsordningen*), governing the organization of the Riksdag and general legislative procedures. Of equal constitutional status but not directly pertaining to structured political relations are the Law on the Freedom of the Press (*Tryckfrihetsförordningen*) and the Act of Succession (*Successionsordningen*). Each of these four documents, which together comprise the Swedish constitution, can be amended only by a majority vote in two successive sessions of the Riksdag with an intervening general election.[2]

As modified by custom and the political realities of majority-minority relations, the rules contained in the Instrument of Government and the Act of Parliament (in conjunction with the Riksdag's own standing orders) provide a comprehensive outline of parliamentary organization and functions. The nation's highest representative structure, the Riksdag "has jurisdiction over the rights and obligations that law accords citizens of the realm."[3] Its formal role in Swedish political processes approximates that of the British parliament, but like the House of Commons the Riksdag is largely subordinate to cabinet domination.

---

[2] The constitutional texts are printed in Robert Malmgren, *Sveriges grundlagar och tillhörande författningar*, 8th ed. (Stockholm: P. A. Norstedts & Söners Förlag, 1964). Data in this chapter on the constitutional amendments of 1967–1969 are derived from *Statens offentliga utredningar 1967:26, Partiell författningsreform* (Stockholm: Justitiedepartementet, 1967). For the sake of brevity in the notes, the Instrument of Government will be referred to by its Swedish abbreviation, RF, while the Act of Parliament is abbreviated as RO.

[3] *RF*, art. 49.

Until the constitutional reform of 1967–1969 took effect on January 1, 1971, the Swedish parliament consisted of two houses of disparate size that shared equal legislative competence. The lower chamber (*andra kammaren*) was popularly elected at four-year intervals, and consisted of 233 members chosen from 28 county and city constituencies. Members of Sweden's 31 provincial and city assemblies, who were similarly elected for terms of four years, selected the 151 representatives in the upper house (*första kammaren*) for staggered individual terms of eight years.[4]

With the introduction of unicameralism the former total membership of 384 deputies has been reduced to 350. Of this number 310 are chosen according to the modified Sainte Lagüe system of proportional representation in 28 individual constituencies. The remaining 40 delegates are elected on a national basis. As previously noted, a party must obtain either 4 percent or 12 percent of the national vote or votes cast in a single constituency, respectively, to win representation in the Riksdag. Terms of office are now three years instead of four. As agreed in the party compromise of 1967, national elections are held simultaneously with communal elections—always in September unless a dissolution election intervenes.

Riksdag candidates must be at least 23 years old. Once they are elected, parliamentary deputies are constitutionally guaranteed immunity from arrest and prosecution. Such immunity may be suspended only upon the affirmative vote of five sevenths of the Riksdag membership.[5]

Legislative officers include the Speaker and three Vice-Speakers. Appointed by the king until 1921, the speakers are now elected by majority vote.[6] Incumbents are usually reelected as long as they wish to remain in office. Custom decrees that the speakers, whose primary function is to preside over plenary sessions of the Riksdag, are chosen among the four major parties. Whenever a vacancy occurs, leaders of the four major parties meet informally to nominate a successor.

To guarantee the impartiality of the legislative officers, the Instrument of Government originally prohibited the presiding speaker from participating in discussions or voting on a particular

---

[4] When the bicameral system was adopted in 1865–1866, the number of lower house deputies was 230. An additional seat was added in 1956, and in 1964 the total was increased to 233. The size of the upper house, originally consisting of 150 members, was increased to 151 in 1956.

[5] *RF*, art. 110.

[6] Standing Orders, art. 6, in Malmgren, pp. 168–169.

parliamentary measures.[7] Because this provision led to a deadlock in the lower house in 1958,[8] the constitution was amended in 1961 to allow the speaker the right to vote.[9]

In addition to their duties as presiding officers, the four speakers serve with four members elected by the Riksdag and the chairmen of the standing committees on the Speakers Conference (*talmanskonferensen*). The Speakers Conference meets at least once a month to coordinate and plan the parliamentary order of business, primarily on the basis of deliberations in progress in the committees.

Effective legislative capacity to examine and possibly amend executive proposals is focused in various standing, special, and combined committees. A distinctive feature of the previous bicameral parliament, one shared by the Norwegian Storting, was that virtually all committees were joint ones composed of an equal number of representatives from each house, thereby imparting an important functional characteristic of unicameralism to the Riksdag. The only exceptions were Special Committees of House Internal Affairs that were formed to consider questions concerning only one of the chambers. Reports from the joint committee were issued simultaneously to both chambers, where they were usually assured of speedy dispatch. Now that bicameralism has been abolished, the committees report directly to parliament as a whole.

The most important committees are the 11 standing committees on foreign affairs, the constitution, supply, ways and means, banking, agriculture, miscellaneous affairs, and four committees on the laws. Another standing group is the Advisory Council on Foreign Affairs (*utrikesnämnd*), created in 1937 and presently composed of seven members appointed by the Riksdag from the committee on foreign affairs. Its purpose is "to confer with the [cabinet] on matters concerning relations of the realm with foreign powers . . ."[10] before the government undertakes any major foreign policy decision. The size of the regular standing committees ranges from 17 members on 8 committees, 27 on 2, and 45 on 1. The second type, special committees, are occasionally appointed to consider matters falling outside the purview of the standing committees. A third kind is the combined committee,

7 *RO*, art. 51. See Malmgren, pp. 174–175.

8 The deadlock occurred during the supplementary pension conflict; see Chapter Eight.

9 Malmgren, p. 175.

10 *RF*, art. 54, and *RO*, art. 49.

which deals with proposed legislation falling within the competence of two of the standing committees.

Committee members and an equal number of alternates are elected at the beginning of each Riksdag session by the plenary body, with prior party caucuses deciding on the nominees. Membership is distributed among the various parties (with the exception of the Left Party-Communists) on the basis of proportional representation. As in the case of the parliamentary speakers, individual members are usually reelected as long as they are willing to serve and their party's strength in the Riksdag entitles them to a seat. Each committee choses its own chairman and vice-chairman. In this instance, too, the positions are proportioned among the four major parties.

Formally the Riksdag is empowered with a comprehensive range of rule-making, control, and supervisory functions. To the first category belong both exclusive and shared legislative jurisdiction. The Riksdag alone has the legal power of taxation[11] and appropriation.[12] It shares with the cabinet the right of constitutional amendment,[13] the right to legislate civil and criminal law,[14] and authority to schedule advisory referenda "on questions of special importance."[15]

At the same time the Riksdag is enjoined from interfering in the autonomous powers of other political structures. Article 90 of the Instrument of Government reads:

> During deliberations of the Riksdag or its committees no questions may be considered other than in instances or ways expressly provided in the constitution concerning the appointment or dismissal of civil servants, decisions of the government or courts, relations between individuals and corporations, or the execution of any law, statute, or enactment.

The purpose of this provision, which dates from the nineteenth century, is not to restrict legislative competence in the manner of the "skrunken domain of the laws" in the French Fifth Republic, but to underscore the functional separation of legislative and executive powers. Conversely, the king may not attend Riksdag and committee deliberations.[16]

[11] *RF*, art. 57.
[12] *RF*, art. 60.
[13] *RF*, art. 81.
[14] *RF*, art. 87.
[15] *RF*, art. 49.
[16] *RF*, art. 55.